WHAT THE VICTORIANS DID FOR US

ADAM HART-DAVIS

headline

First published in 2001
by HEADLINE BOOK PUBLISHING
First published in 2001
by HEADLINE BOOK PUBLISHING

By arrangement with the BBC

The BBC logo and the 'What the Victorians Did for Us' logo are trade marks of the British Broadcasting Corporation and are used under licence

BBC logo © BBC 1996
'What the Victorians Did for Us' logo © 2001

10 9 8 7 6 5 4 3 2 1

ISBN 0 7553 1137 X

Designed by Harry Green
Edited by Colin Grant
Printed and bound in Great Britain by Butler and Tanner

Every effort has been made to fulfil requirements with regard to reproducing copyright material. The author and publisher will be glad to rectify any omissions at the earliest opportunity.

HEADLINE BOOK PUBLISHING
A division of Hodder Headline
338 Euston Road
London NW1 3BH

www.headline.co.uk
www.hodderheadline.com

BY THE SAME AUTHOR

Don't Just Sit There!

Where There's Life… (with Hilary Lawson)

Scientific Eye

Mathematical Eye

World's Weirdest 'True' Ghost Stories

Test Your Psychic Powers (with Susan Blackmore)

Thunder, Flush, and Thomas Crapper

Science Tricks

The Local Heroes Book of British Ingenuity (with Paul Bader)

Amazing Math Puzzles

More Local Heroes (with Paul Bader)

Eurekaaargh! – Inventions that Nearly Worked

Local Heroes DIY Science (with Paul Bader)

Henry Winstanley and the Eddystone Lighthouse (with Emily Troscianko)

PAGE 2
'The Triumph of Steam and Electricity' from the 1897 Jubilee edition of the *Illustrated London News*, showing how transport had progressed during Victoria's reign, with portraits of important figures in the field.

CONTENTS

INTRODUCTION

ALEXANDRINA VICTORIA WAS BORN on 24 May 1819 at Kensington Palace in London's Hyde Park, and on 20 June 1837 – less than a month after her eighteenth birthday – she became Queen Victoria. She succeeded her uncle William IV, who had no surviving legitimate heirs, even though before his marriage to Princess Adelaide he had lived for many years with the glamorous actress Dora Jordan, and they had ten children together, of whom the sixth, Elizabeth, was my great-great-great-grandmother. I think that makes Victoria my first cousin, five times removed!

Victoria had an unhappy childhood, but found lasting contentment in the arms of her first cousin, Prince Albert of Saxe-Coburg-Gotha, whom she married on 10 February 1840. They had nine children and were constantly together until he died of typhoid in 1861.

The Victorian era was a time of extraordinary prosperity and development in Britain, for several reasons. First, Victoria reigned for more than sixty years. Second, when she came to the throne the country's economy had just recovered from the disastrous Napoleonic wars, which had ended in 1815. Third, the scientific renaissance of the seventeenth century and the industrial revolution of the eighteenth century had made Britain the world leader in steam engines and iron and steel produc-

The Secret of England's Greatness (Queen Victoria presenting a Bible in the Audience Chamber at Windsor), *c.*1863 (detail), by Thomas J. Barker, with Prince Albert behind. The Victorians were determined to guide poor, uneducated people to Christianity and morality.

tion. Tremendous wealth was created in the cotton and woollen mills, which in turn helped to drive vast expansion in international trade. This explosion of power, pride and progress was celebrated in the Great Exhibition of 1851.

Britain acquired an empire; industrialists saw their horizons ever-widening; engineers believed that with steam and steel they could build anything; and scientists discovered whole new fields of nature to investigate. Indeed, the word 'scientist' was coined by the Cambridge polymath William Whewell, who wrote in 1840: 'We need very much a name to describe cultivator of science in general. I should incline to call him a scientist.' The following year Whewell became master of Trinity College, and the story goes that while he was showing the Queen round Cambridge they walked by the River Cam, into which all the sewers in the town discharged. Curious, she asked what were all the pieces of paper floating in the river. Quick as a flash he replied, 'Those, Ma'am, are notices saying that bathing is forbidden!'

The state of the sewage in London was even more disgusting, for the population was growing rapidly and the drains were hopelessly inadequate. During the long hot summer of 1858 the smell became intolerable, and the Great Stink was debated in parliament. As a result the Metropolitan Board of Works was given £3 million, and Joseph Bazalgette built the superb network of intercepting sewers that still keep the capital clean. This ushered in the golden age of the water-closet, since middle-class households now had the ways and means to install them. Thousands of water-closet patents were taken out, and plumbers like George Jennings and Thomas Crapper became rich and famous.

During the same decade William Budd and John Snow had shown that the dreadful diseases typhoid and cholera were transmitted through contamination of the water supply, so the introduction of clean piped water was a giant step forward in health. John Snow was also one of the pioneers of anaesthetics in the country, and popularised the practice when he gave the Queen chloroform for the birth of Prince Leopold in 1853. The advent of anaesthetics and antiseptic surgery allowed surgeons to operate slowly and become scientists rather than butchers, and so ushered in a new era of scientific medicine.

In 1842 the Queen travelled from Windsor to London by train, much enjoying this spectacular new method of transport. When she came to the throne the railways ran for only a few hundred miles, but during her reign they spread not only across the country but around the world, changing public transport for ever. Meanwhile the roads had improved considerably since the pioneering work of Thomas Telford and John Loudon McAdam earlier in the century, so getting about the country became steadily easier.

Communications also took off. Mechanical telegraphs had been used during the Napoleonic wars, but they were little more than improved versions of Roman signalling systems. However, the electric telegraph, growing alongside the railways, allowed messages to be transmitted instantaneously along wires. The Queen was much amused by this, had her own telegraph system installed at Buckingham Palace, and delighted in sending messages to the Empire, for cables were laid across the Atlantic and all the way to India in what was essentially a Victorian Internet.

The middle classes appeared, and acquired spare time and spare cash. Armed with the new lawn-mower, they invented games like lawn tennis, and made rules for old ones like football. They dreamed up weekends, package holidays, ice cream, seaside piers, pianolas and musical boxes, and even the traditions of Christmas.

This book, following the BBC2 television series, is a celebration of that unparalleled growth and development. The Victorian age laid the foundations for our own; indeed, much of the world we live in is Victorian. I live in a Victorian house and cycle along Victorian roads, riding what is in essence a Victorian cycle; I travel to London on the Great Western Railway, built by Isambard Kingdom Brunel.

If we could resurrect a Victorian family, they would recognise most of the hardware of our world, apart from the fancy electronic gadgets – television, computers and mobile phones – and the cars and trucks dominating the roads. They would probably be impressed and a little scared by the pace of modern existence; in some ways Victorian life must have been slower and more peaceful; I think I would rather put up with the clatter of horses' hoofs on cobbles than with the thundering of today's diesel engines.

The central idea of this book, as of the television programmes, is to take you back to visit that Victorian world which became our own, to see how their institutions and practices developed into the life we have today, and to get some idea of what it must have been like to live in Victorian Britain. I hope you enjoy reading it as much as I have enjoyed writing it and presenting the series.

ADAM HART-DAVIS
July 2001

CHAPTER ONE

SPEED MERCHANTS

FOR THOUSANDS OF YEARS the galloping horse must have seemed the limit of speed, the fastest anyone could travel, thundering through the countryside at perhaps 25 miles per hour, or even faster over short distances. This changed dramatically in the 1830s, as Victoria came to the throne. Even the primitive railway locomotive *Rocket*, built by Robert Stephenson for the Rainhill Trials in 1829, managed a sustained speed of 15 miles per hour and a breathtaking top speed of 29 – almost three times as fast as one of the judges had considered possible. By 1837 speeds of 50 or 60 were being achieved, in spite of dire warnings that travelling at any such speed would cause instant death by suffocation, since the air would undoubtedly be sucked out of the lungs.

The unofficial speed record for the fist half of the nineteenth century was probably held by a student called Frank Ebrington, riding on the atmospheric railway test track near Dublin. The carriages of the atmospheric railway were pulled not by a locomotive but by a piston travelling along inside a tube between the rails. Steam engines pumped the air from this tube in front of the train, and the pressure of the atmosphere behind it pushed the piston along. The piston was connected to the carriage by an iron rod passing through the top of the tube. Ebrington climbed aboard the first carriage, thinking that five more were connected behind him. He was mistaken. When he released the brake the entire pull of the piston was applied to his carriage alone, and he was hauled up a mile and a half of sharply twisting track at an average speed of 84 miles per hour, which must have been utterly terrifying.

The South Devon Railway at Dawlish. Brunel built his atmospheric railway right beside the sea, down the estuary from Exeter and up past Teignmouth to Newton Abbot. The 'campanile' tower hides the boiler chimney for the Dawlish pumping station. Note the 15 inch cast-iron pipe between the rails.

THE ATMOSPHERIC RAILWAY

Isambard Kingdom Brunel built an atmospheric railway between Exeter and Newton Abbot, and it ran for nearly a year from September 1847.

The passengers loved it, for the absence of a locomotive meant no noise, no smoke, no smuts and no fiery sooty fragments to burn holes in their clothes. But above all the trains were fast. They leaped away from the platform with exciting acceleration, because they were much lighter than trains with locomotives. Speeds of 50 miles per hour were common, and on one run the train travelled the 20 miles from Newton Abbot to Exeter in twenty-two minutes, which is faster than intercity trains do it today.

However, Brunel never solved the problem of two lines meeting in a simple Y-junction. The carriages on one branch would have to jump over the tube on the other branch; but there could be no gap in the tube, or there would be no vacuum.

The Liverpool–
Manchester
Railway. Each first-
class 'coach' (above)
consists essentially
of three carriages
bolted together.
The second-class
carriages (below)
have no roofs; so the
'outside passengers'
are exposed to rain,
steam, smoke, soot
and burning fiery
fragments from the
chimney.

There was also trouble with the seal in the top of the tube. The iron
rod connecting the piston to the carriage came out through a slot along
the top of the tube. This slot was 3 inches wide, and was closed by a
leather flap that was designed to maintain the vacuum but was lifted to
allow the rod to pass along. Unfortunately this leather flap froze hard in
winter, while in summer it dried out. In both cases the stiff leather made a
poor seal; so men had to walk along the line painting the leather with a
mixture of lime soap and whale oil, but the oil attracted rats, the rats ate
the leather, and the vacuum was never good. The Boulton & Watt steam
engines had to be kept running continuously to keep the pressure low, and
this was far too expensive. In the end there was a financial scandal; by a
piece of creative accounting some of the atmospheric system's detractors
managed to demonstrate that the South Devon Railway had made a loss
in its first year of operation, and the shareholders voted it out.

GOD'S WONDERFUL RAILWAY

The South Devon atmospheric railway was probably the most expensive disaster in engineering history – it cost the shareholders half a million pounds – but the rest of the railway system was an astonishing success. The first real passenger railway opened between Liverpool and Manchester in 1830; by 1837 about 500 miles of railway had been built, and by 1850 more than 6,000. The first great railway engineer was George Stephenson, who with his son Robert acquired almost a monopoly on the early railways in the north of England. However, the most flamboyant of the railway builders was Isambard Kingdom Brunel.

When Thomas Guppy and other merchant venturers of Bristol first raised the idea of building a railway to London, because they needed to compete with Liverpool, they decided to invite several engineers to survey routes and estimate the total cost of the railway; they would then choose the cheapest. Brunel, already arrogant at the age of twenty-seven, said he would not compete in such a Dutch auction; he wrote: 'The route I survey will not be the cheapest – but it will be the best.' This attitude did not go down well with the committee, but it won him the job, by a single vote.

As the engineer in charge of Britain's biggest railway project – it was to become the Great Western Railway – Isambard Kingdom Brunel was in his element. He rode hundreds of miles on horseback seeking out the best route, along the River Avon to Bath, up over the hills to Chippenham, across remote grassland to Swindon, and then into the Thames Valley at Reading. Trains still follow the route he surveyed, although the GWR is not often called God's Wonderful Railway today!

The first GWR passengers were carried on 31 May 1838, just before the coronation. Three hundred guests left Paddington at 11.30 a.m. and steamed along at an impressive 28 miles per hour to reach Maidenhead forty-nine minutes later. After a colossal celebratory luncheon, at which many toasts were drunk, they travelled back at an average of 33 miles per hour, and Thomas Guppy, one of those responsible for the whole under-taking, walked along the top of the train while it heaved and lurched along the uneven track.

The ride had been generally bumpy for Isambard. He had to persuade the shareholders that his estimate of two and a half million pounds for the GWR was reasonable, and then in the end he had to explain why the actual cost was almost three times as much. He had to do battle with unwilling landowners. He had to build several challenging bridges, some of which his critics thought would not last the winter. He had to cope with scientific sniping from the celebrated Dr Dionysius Lardner, who disagreed on many fundamental points. He had to cope with several other major projects that were happening at the same time – he was building a huge ship, the *Great Western*, in Bristol, the Clifton Suspension Bridge and several other small railways. But above all he had to cope with the terrain.

His critics were particularly fierce about what they called his 'monstrous and extraordinary, most dangerous and impracticable' tunnel at Box. Box is 6 miles east of Bath, and Brunel decided to tunnel through the hill immediately east of Box. The tunnel was to be almost 2 miles long, sloping down towards the west with a gradient of one in a hundred. Dionysius Lardner calculated that if the train's brakes failed as it entered the tunnel from the east, it would emerge at Box at 120 miles per hour, which would suffocate all the passengers by sucking all the air from their

The 'monstrous and extraordinary, most dangerous and impractical' tunnel at Box.

lungs. Professor William Buckland (see p. 54) said that the vibration caused by a train passing through might bring the entire roof of the tunnel down on top of it. Even the digging was bad enough.

The shafts dug down through the hill to provide ventilation filled up with water, and pumping out the water emptied the contractors' pockets faster than the shafts. The east end of the tunnel ran through soft clay and had to be lined with thirty million bricks. The west end went through hard Bath stone; every week the 1,200 navvies working on it used a ton of gunpowder for blasting and a ton of candles for lighting. A hundred horses dragged away the earth and stone. And the tunnel was certainly dangerous: a hundred men died during the construction. All you can now see, looking from the bridge over the line at the western end, is a modest stone archway in the side of the hill.

The Great Western Railway reached Bristol in 1841 and brought to the West Country a new concept of transport: to be able to travel from Bristol to London in four hours was amazing; for the first time a businessman could go to London and be back the same day. However, the journey was not entirely wonderful. There were no lavatories on the train, and the only chance the passengers had to relieve themselves was at Swindon, where every train stopped for just ten minutes. The local facilities were quite inadequate, and there are stories of the men congregating at one end of the platform and the women at the other, all pretending to admire the view.

The catering facilities were also less than perfect; perhaps it was at Swindon station that railway refreshments first got their dreadful reputation. Brunel was running way over budget, and had to let the management of the hotel and restaurant at Swindon station on a long-term contract. The dining room was immensely elegant, and enticed hundreds of passengers in, but few were satisfied. The soup with which they were served was literally boiling, so that there was no chance of even the first arrivals drinking it within ten minutes; when the train had gone, the staff would allegedly go round collecting the near-full bowls and tip the contents back into the tureen. Brunel himself wrote an angry letter to the proprietor, which ended: 'I did not believe you had such a thing as coffee in the place. I certainly never tasted any. I have long ceased to make complaints at Swindon. I avoid taking anything there when I can help it.'

CHANGING TIME

For all their faults, the railways revolutionised Britain. One of the unexpected consequences of such rapid travel was the necessity for universal time. Before the coming of the railways, each town had its own time, specified by the clock on the church or the town hall. But the railways changed all that. I like to think the problem surfaced first in Bristol, where people kept missing trains. They would turn up at Temple Meads Station at five to eleven in order to catch the eleven o'clock train, and find it had already left. Why? Because Bristol time was ten or eleven minutes behind London time – being further west, Bristol sees the sunrise later – and the engine drivers used London time. The solution was for everyone to change over to what was called 'railway time'. The guard would use his watch to check the time at each stop, and the station clock became the reference point for each town. Reactionaries in Oxford hung out as long as they could, and for some years the clock on Tom Tower at Christchurch College had two minute-hands set five minutes apart – one for Oxford time and one for railway time.

REACHING FOR THE SKY

When it first arrived, the railway must have seemed little short of a miracle – the puffing monsters of the steam engines, and the glorious sensation of speed without the exertion of any muscle-power. Some people, however, were not content to keep their feet on the ground and were determined to follow the birds into the air.

In 1783 the Montgolfier brothers had flown a hot-air balloon over Paris, and in one splendid demonstration galvanised the dreamers of the world into believing that true flight might be possible – flight in which people might be able to soar like birds, controlling their direction and speed, and land with safety wherever they wished. One of those so inspired was the nine-year-old George Cayley, who lived at Brompton near Scarborough in north Yorkshire, and in 1792 succeeded his father to become the sixth baronet, Sir George Cayley. He was a busy landowner with a lifelong interest in science and technology: he invented cowcatchers and seatbelts for trains, and rifled shells; he drained his land; but above all he studied flight.

Sir George Cayley's paper on the world's first man-carrying aircraft, which he curiously called a 'governable parachute'.

He watched crows, measured how fast they flapped their wings and noted especially that, when they stopped flapping, they did not plummet to the ground but were able to glide for considerable distances. This was a vital observation, because Cayley realised, unlike previous would-be aviators, that the crows could get lift without flapping their wings. Therefore he abandoned his early experiments with ornithopters and concentrated on fixed-wing aircraft.

He devised a wonderful whirling-arm machine, and used it to investigate the effect on lift of varying the wing size, shape and especially the 'angle of attack'. He came to the conclusion that the wing should be tilted upwards at an angle of about six degrees. This angle of attack is astonishingly close to what is used in today's aircraft. He wrote up his aeronautical experiments in *Mechanics' Magazine*, and when the Wright brothers flew at Kitty Hawk in 1903, they paid him a handsome tribute, saying he had 'carried the science of flying to a point which it had never reached before, and which it scarcely reached again during the last century'.

Finally, after many years of experimenting, Cayley built a glider big enough to carry a man, and since he was then seventy-nine – rather old to learn to fly – he volunteered his coachman John Appleby to be the world's first test-pilot. One day in the summer of 1853 the aircraft was hauled up to one side of the little valley opposite the house. Six farm-hands pulling on ropes ran down the slope and launched the machine into the air. It flew some 200 yards across the valley and landed heavily below the trees on the other side. The coachman crawled from the wreckage and said: 'Sir George, I wish to give notice. I was hired to drive, not to fly!' This was the first flight by a man in a heavier-than-air flying machine.

Cayley's aircraft was only a glider, but he hoped to build a powered aircraft and even experimented with a gunpowder engine, knowing that to keep an aircraft flying would need a high power-to-weight ratio. He lamented that powered flight would not be possible 'until we can get a hundred horsepower into a pint pot'. He was almost right; genuinely controlled sustained flight became possible only with the arrival of the internal combustion engine, since the steam engine would always be too heavy for the amount of power it could deliver. However, there was one extraordinary man who managed to get a steam-powered aircraft to fly.

John Stringfellow was born in Attercliff, on the edge of Sheffield, on 6 December 1799. He went with his family to Nottingham, joined the lace business and became a bobbin-and-carriage maker, which in essence meant a skilled engineer, since the bobbin-and-carriage was an intricate part of the lace-making machine, and some machines needed hundreds of them to function. When lace-making in Nottingham was disturbed by Luddites, Stringfellow moved to the calmer area of Somerset and went on making lace there.

In his spare time he also made miniature steam engines and became fascinated by the possibility of flying. He launched a hot-air balloon to celebrate the coronation of William IV in 1831, and he joined forces with one Samuel Henson to try and build aircraft. Following Cayley, they focused on fixed-wing aircraft; on one occasion Stringfellow spun a sheet of cardboard across the room and said 'any surface will hold the air with applied power'. They borrowed a muzzle-loading duck-gun and went

The press were immensely scornful of Samuel Henson's grand plans to build a large passenger-carrying aircraft and launch an airline.

round shooting every bird they could find, in order to measure their weights and wing areas, and to try and discover some guiding principles. Cayley studied crows; Stringfellow said:

> Henson and me generally took the rook as our standard as carrying half a pound to a (square) foot. This bird can be seen any day leisurely flying at a speed not more than twenty miles an hour, and we considered that if we kept our machine within these limits we had a fair chance of success.

In 1843 Henson ambitiously tried not only to patent an aircraft but also to set up an airline, and became the butt of press ridicule. The idea of people flying about as passengers seemed too absurd to take seriously. Eventually this fierce criticism became too much for Henson; he married, moved to New York and patented a safety razor. Stringfellow was left to carry on alone.

By the summer of 1848 he had built a new aircraft, a model with a 10

Stringfellow Flies Again?

Using modern technology, but only the same materials as were available to John Stringfellow, can a group of engineering apprentices at Rolls-Royce build a replica Stringfellow aircraft and get it to fly?

They started with several handicaps. For one thing most of the engineering techniques of today rely on modern materials and specified tolerances, while Stringfellow worked with intuition and his knowledge of this particular batch of copper sheet. He made his boiler a curious shape with conical vessels designed to minimise both the amount of water the aircraft would have to carry and the time needed to boil the water. The apprentices found this construction tricky – especially getting steam-tight seals between the tubes at the bottom, which meet in a V-shape.

Stringfellow's boiler was paper-thin, to keep the weight down; when filled with steam at high pressure, it must have been seriously dangerous. Today the apprentices have to fulfil the stringent requirements of the Health and Safety Executive, which means a thicker and therefore heavier boiler.

The copper boiler with its V-shaped conical vessels (below). Checking the balance of the aircraft with its engine-carrying 'gondola' (right).

Discussing the challenge with Rolls-Royce's chief test pilot (above). The apprentices testing the steam engine on the bench (right).

Making the wings and tail from spars of spruce covered with silk – following Stringfellow's original design – was not a great problem; these engineers know a great deal more than he did about flight. However, Stringfellow was a genius at building small steam engines, where today's apprentices have no experience whatever. This was their downfall – on the day of the first trial they could not get the steam engine running well enough to drive the aircraft. The machine launched itself perfectly from the guide wire, the propellers would spin, but in the end the aircraft would not quite fly under its own power.

foot wingspan. The fuselage and wings were made from spruce and other wooden spars, covered with silk. The tiny steam engine had a 2 inch cylinder with a stroke of about 2 inches, and a paper-thin copper boiler to provide the steam. Stringfellow decided to go for a maiden flight inside the lace mill, where the damp and the wind would not interfere with the flight.

His aircraft did not have a fin or other system for lateral stability – after all, nor do rooks. So he knew that he had to make sure the machine was launched straight and level, to avoid turning sharply one way or the other, and breaking a wing on the ground. To make matters more challenging, the wingspan was 10 feet, and the flight path was only 20 feet wide between the wall of the mill and the row of cast-iron pillars down the middle. So there was only 5 feet of clearance between the wingtip and a devastating obstacle.

He launched his aircraft down a wire, which sloped down for half the length of the mill. The plan was to start the engine at one end, and set the machine off so that it would slide down the wire, gathering speed, and by the time it released itself at the end of the wire it would already be at flying speed (about 15 miles per hour) and flying dead straight and level, with no tendency to veer left or right. The only description of the flight was written down many years later by his fourth son John (always known as Fred to avoid confusion!):

> In the first experiment the tail was set at too high an angle, and the machine rose too rapidly on leaving the wire. After going a few yards it slid back, as if coming down an inclined plane at such an angle that the point of the tail struck the ground and was broken. The tail was repaired and set at a less angle. The steam was again got up, the machine started down the wire and upon reaching the point of self-detachment, gradually rose until it reached the farther end of the room, striking a hole in the canvas placed to stop it.

THE DARK SATANIC MILLS

Thomas Newcomen, Dartmouth ironmonger, built the world's first useful steam engine in 1712 to pump the water from a coal mine at Dudley in the West Midlands, and this was one of the greatest advances in technology, because it enabled people to have power wherever they wanted it without relying on animal muscle. For more than fifty years steam engines were used only to pump water from mines, but in the 1780s James Watt made engines that were more effective and could be used to drive rotating machinery. When James Watt's patent ran out in 1800, the way was clear for others, notably Richard Trevithick, to begin experimenting with high-pressure steam engines, and because these were far more efficient, they could be made much smaller and lighter, and were therefore mobile. Trevithick built a steam carriage in 1801 and a steam locomotive to pull a train three years later. Within thirty years the railways were crawling across the country, and steam engines began to appear in the mills.

For centuries people had used water wheels to provide power for machinery. In 1771 Richard Arkwright built a substantial mill at Cromford in Derbyshire in order to spin cotton, using his patented 'water-frame', so called because it was driven by power from a water wheel. Before then, spinning had been a skilled task for a spinster making one thread with a spinning wheel or up to a dozen with a spinning jenny – but this was very tricky to operate. Arkwright's water-frame turned spinning into child's play, and he employed children to mind the machines, on which one unskilled teenager could

Women in a mill with steam-powered sewing machines (*c.*1875).

spin ninety-six threads simultaneously. Arkwright earned himself a knighthood and a vast fortune (see p. 176), and laid the foundations for the immense growth of the cotton and woollen industries, and the wealth of Manchester, Leeds and other northern textile towns.

As the production of threads mushroomed, the demand for weaving grew with it, and Edmund Cartwright's power loom provided the answer. However, there were not enough rivers in Lancashire and Yorkshire to provide water power for all the new mills – Oldham alone boasted almost one mill for every day of the year – and so the mill steam engine came into its own. By 1837 Trevithick's 'Cornish' engines were ten times as efficient as the old Newcomen or 'common' engines, and the fact that they provided constant reliable power made them highly desirable to mill-owners. Typically one huge steam engine on the ground floor or in the basement of the mill would provide power to rotating shafts running along below the ceiling in each floor of the mill. From these shafts power could be taken by means of belts to every machine that needed it. So one steam engine could drive hundreds of machines, with a variety of functions.

Each of the three weaving sheds at Queen Street Mill in Burnley had 300 looms, driven by belts from rotating shafts above. When they were all running the noise must have been ear-splitting.

The steam engine, and the overhead shafts, turned all day, but individual machines often needed to be started and stopped. When you wanted to start your machine you had to knock the drive belt from a loose (freewheeling) pulley on to the fixed or 'fast' one, which then transmitted the drive to your machine. These twin pulleys were called 'fast' and 'loose'.

Working in the mills must have meant long days on your feet and probably a dull repetitive task. Furthermore, the mill managers wanted efficiency, and that meant discipline; you had to stay by your machines, not go wandering about and chatting to the other workers, and above all you had to arrive on time in the morning, and clock in. If anything could embody an idea, this was it – time was money, speed was king, and your life was driven by the machines in the factory. If you were late, the mill-owner might well lock the factory gates and you would lose your day's wages.

Even if you arrived on time the work was hard. You were paid a fixed amount for a 'piece' of cloth – usually about ten yards by perhaps a yard

wide. These came to be called 'piece rates'. However, at least you kept dry and reasonably warm, and you were paid at the end of the week. They may have looked dark and satanic to some, but to many thousands the mills represented progress, and working there must have been better than tramping about the countryside looking for casual labour on the farms. At one period there were 100,000 looms in Burnley alone, and literally millions in Lancashire. The wealth of the county, and of Manchester in particular, was based on this colossal cotton industry. It thrived in Lancashire because the damp air was just right for the cotton threads, while the wool industry settled over the Pennines in Yorkshire.

QUEEN STREET MILL

Queen Street Mill in Burnley is the only remaining steam-powered cotton-weaving mill in Britain. Officially it closed in 1982, but it was kept open as a museum and still produces a small amount of cotton cloth, including Victorian-style shirting and prayer shawls for the Middle East. The magnificent 500-horsepower steam engine was called Prudence when the mill was originally built in 1894, but was renamed Peace at the end of the First World War in 1918. This engine drove – and still drives – all the machinery in the mill through overhead shafts that run the length and breadth of the building.

The mill had three weaving sheds, with 300 looms in each. A single loom makes a tremendous racket as the shuttle crashes to and fro carrying the weft, and with 300 running the noise in the sheds must have been shattering. There was no question of the weavers being able to talk to one another – they communicated in their own sign language – and every chance of permanent damage to their hearing. Each weaver was expected to look after six looms, which was a tough job, stopping each machine every minute or two to slip in a new spindle of weft before the old one ran out, and rescuing any disasters, such as breakage of warp threads; there was never a chance of sitting down on the job.

INDUSTRIAL AGRICULTURE

To say that the Victorians were obsessed with speed would be unfair. On the whole the movers and shakers were more interested in power – political power, financial power and sheer horsepower for moving machinery. Before 1800 life on the farm moved at the pace of the carthorse – the ploughman homeward plodded his weary way – but agriculture was not immune to industrial progress. Gradually the idea of steam power invaded the countryside, and when it did, the change brought about by the steam engine was as dramatic on the farm as in the factory.

The plough had scarcely evolved since Roman times, and even in the 1850s there were plenty of wooden ploughs in use in Britain, although farmers were increasingly taking to clever iron self-sharpening ploughshares and steel mould-boards that turned over the sticky earth rather than dragging it across the field. But then came total revolution, in the shape of the Fowler steam plough introduced in the 1850s.

At the Chester Show of 1858 John Fowler, born at Melksham in Wiltshire, won the Royal Agricultural Society's £500 prize for 'a steam cultivator that shall, in the most efficient manner, turn over the soil and be an economic substitute for the plough or the spade'. His idea was to place a large stationary steam engine in the field, and use ropes to pull the

A demonstration of the Fowler steam plough in action.

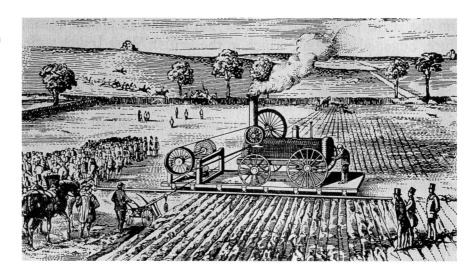

ploughshare up and down. Even though a ploughman might have to guide it, there would be no horse or heavy machinery to turn the field to mud, as so often happened in the winter. The result was a saving in labour costs and better soil for cultivation. The disadvantages were that the great steam engines were heavy enough to sink irretrievably into soft ground, so a hard strip had to be maintained at the end of or across the middle of each field. They were too expensive for small farmers to afford; the only hope was to rent them. And as they reduced labour costs so they created unemployment.

Using the Fowler system to harrow a field. The driver sitting on the harrow is pulled first one way and then the other by a pair of traction engines; his job is to steer the harrow and to help control the turns at each end of the field.

Steam-powered reaping machines, threshing machines – Ransomes won a prize for one from the Royal Agricultural Society in 1842 – and traction engines became important tools for Victorian farmers and were not superseded for fifty years, until the invention of the internal-combustion engine allowed the development of the lightweight tractor. Even then the transition was slow; I was brought up on a farm, and I can just remember from the late 1940s the arrival of the great lumbering traction engine for the process of threshing the corn.

SEA POWER

The earliest steam engines were too big and heavy to be useful for transport, but by the end of the eighteenth century they had become small and light enough to be tried out in boats, which could carry the weight without having the railway engine's problem of breaking up the track underneath. Experiments in France, in Scotland and in America led to the construction of successful paddle-steamers. The idea of the paddle-boat followed logically from the use of oars and paddles – wooden blades pushing the water back one after another – and the Romans had written about an ox-powered paddle ship in the third century AD. However, the beginning of Victoria's reign saw the invention of a new and clever device, the screw propeller.

With hindsight we know that propellers are efficient, but there is no propeller in nature – fish and ducks use a form of paddle propulsion rather than screw – so the idea had to be quite new, although perhaps the fact that the Archimedes screw had been used for hundreds of years to pump water along pipes might have provided a clue. Robert Hooke suggested the use of a screw propeller in 1681, and in 1795 Joseph Bramah took out a patent, although apparently he never made one. An American called John Cox Stevens and a Swede called John Ericsson both experimented with propellers around 1800.

On 28 June 1834 the Revd Edward Lyon Berthon, Rector of Romsey Abbey in Hampshire, was sketching on a ferry on Lake Geneva, when a blob of water flicked up by the paddle wheel landed right on his sketchpad and ruined his picture. He was naturally irritated by this and reasoned that it was not only annoying but must also be inefficient: the power of the engine should all be used to push the boat forward, not to throw water into the air.

He wondered whether a boat could be propelled by a screw. After all, a screw pulls its way through wood, so why should not a screw pull its way through water? He decided to test his idea, so back home in Romsey he dug a circular pond in his garden, made a model boat that would cruise round and round, and constructed a screw to propel it. He reckoned that to get a good grip on the water he would need five or six turns of the screw thread. The screw worked, and did push the boat around, but when he tried shortening the screw the boat went faster. He made it shorter and shorter until what he called his 'screw propeller' had only one sixth of a turn, and his boat zoomed around the pond. Then, bursting with pride and enthusiasm, he took his model boat to the Admiralty in London and suggested they might be interested. They looked at it with contempt and said that it was a pretty toy, but it never could and never would power a real ship.

Berthon was probably annoyed by this rejection, and no doubt even more annoyed when an enthusiastic builder of model boats called Francis Pettit Smith invented his own screw propeller in 1835 and put an improved version on display in 1836. Both Smith and Ericsson took out patents in 1837, and after Smith had built a 10 ton boat and driven her round successfully with a propeller the Admiralty at last began to pay attention. A small company was formed, and they built a 237 ton screw steamer, appropriately called the *Archimedes*, with a steam engine of 80 horsepower. The Admiralty declared they would be satisfied if the *Archimedes* could cruise at 5 knots; in practice she managed 10. She also outperformed the *Vulcan*, one of the fastest paddle-steamers in Her Majesty's service. Eventually a trial was arranged – a genuine scientific experiment – to see whether the paddle or the screw was more efficient.

PADDLE OR SCREW?

While Brunel was still investigating the effectiveness of the propeller using *Archimedes*, two other ships were compared in the most direct way – a tug of war. The *Alecto* and the *Rattler* were sloops of similar design and size, and had similar engines, but the *Alecto* was fitted with paddle wheels while the *Rattler* had a screw propeller. They were tied together, stern to stern, with a towrope, and then both engines were put to 'Full ahead'. To the surprise of most of the onlookers, the *Rattler* pulled the *Alecto* backwards at almost three knots.

We wanted to find out whether this would really work, so we fitted out two identical canoes, one with paddles and the other with screw propellers. These were carefully designed and built so that the same area of blade would be in the water for each boat. The tug of war was held in the harbour at Bristol, only 100 yards from the *Great Britain*, and the 'engines' were Scott and Tim, from the City of Bristol Rowing Club. There was a strong wind, perhaps Force 5, blowing down the harbour, and as an added handicap we made Tim, driving a screw propeller in the *Rattler*, go upwind. We estimated that without any artificial propulsion the boats drifted with the wind at about 3 or 4 knots.

On the command 'Ready, steady, ROW!' both the engines applied maximum power, and the towrope tautened, springing out of the water. For a few seconds there was nothing to choose between the boats. Both rowers worked furiously, and spray flew from the paddles, although the propellers were out of sight. However, the *Rattler* gradually began to pull away, and after perhaps twenty seconds had advanced perhaps a metre. Then the contest became progressively more unequal. Once the paddle-boat began to be pulled backwards, Scott found it harder and harder to

The great tug of war (below) between *Rattler* (on the right) and *Alecto* in 1845, and our version of the event (above). In both events the screw propeller proved much more effective than the paddle wheels.

paddle, and Tim seemed to gather speed. Quite clearly the propellers were more effective, under these conditions of maximum load and minimum speed.

After the match, Scott said that cruising about on his own had been easy, but once the towing started he found the paddles extremely hard to turn. Tim said he was really confident, and was impressed by the way that his propellers really seemed to bite into the water, even under load. The tug of war convinced Brunel and the Admiralty. Having been denied any credit for his invention, Berthon had the satisfaction of living to see all the ships in the navy driven by screw propellers.

William Richardson's 'Improved Swimming Device' of 1880.

SWIMMER POWER

The Victorians were immensely fond of gadgets, and I was not surprised during my research to come across various patents for devices to improve your swimming speed. Curiously enough, one of these was for 'paddles' and the other for a screw propeller.

Liborio Pedrazzolli, an Italian immigrant who settled in north London around 1880, married a local girl and made a living selling mirrors, invented swimming umbrellas in 1896. As he explained in his patent, 'The apparati close when the hands are thrust forward thereby causing but little resistance or obstruction … but when the return stroke is made the apparati expand in umbrella form, and the resistance thus offered enables the swimmer to pull or propel himself through the water at a speed hitherto impossible.'

Meanwhile William Richardson's Improved Swimming Device of 1880 transferred the work from the hands and feet to the propeller, which he claimed enabled the swimmer to proceed rapidly and easily, at a speed of 4–6 miles per hour. I only wish Mr Pedrazzolli and Mr Richardson had seized the opportunity to test their devices with a tug of war, tethered to one another by a line tied around their waists, like the *Alecto* and the *Rattler*!

THE GREAT SHIPS

Meanwhile merchant ships were developing too, and Brunel's ventures into shipbuilding demonstrate some of the advances and pitfalls of that complex craft. Late in 1835 the directors of the Great Western Railway met at Radley's Hotel in Blackfriars, and one of them wondered aloud whether the proposed GWR was too long and therefore too ambitious. At this point Brunel is said to have jumped to his feet and said: 'No no; on the contrary – it's not nearly long enough! I'll build a steamship, call her the *Great Western*, and she can cross the Atlantic. Then passengers can buy a ticket all the way from Paddington to New York!' Ironically, this is now possible, although today the route goes from Paddington to Heathrow and then takes to the air. Even though Brunel was half joking, some of the directors took the idea seriously and eventually floated the Great Western Steamship Company. Two of these men, Tom Guppy and Captain Christopher Claxton, were to become lifelong friends and allies of Brunel.

There was tremendous controversy about using steamships to cross the Atlantic. Steam had been used only on boats going up and down the coast, where coal supplies were available. Clearly there would be no coal dump in mid-Atlantic, and so any coal-powered ship would have to carry enough for the whole crossing. The celebrated Dr Dionysius Lardner visited Bristol in August 1836 for the annual meeting of the British Association for the Advancement of Science, and gave a lecture on steam navigation of the Atlantic. He asserted that there was no way a steamship could get from Bristol to New York without picking up more coal on the way. His calculations showed that even if the entire ship was full of coal, with no room for cargo or passengers, she could steam only 2,500 miles, and he concluded: 'Making a voyage directly from New York to Liverpool was perfectly chimerical, and they might as well talk of making a voyage from New York or Liverpool to the moon.'

However, his calculations were based on the assumption that the resistance to a ship's movement through the water was directly proportional to her displacement, so that a 400 ton ship would need twice as much force to push her at a given speed as a 200 ton ship. Brunel had seen the fallacy in this argument and had pointed out: 'The resistance of vessels on the water does not increase in direct proportion to their tonnage. The tonnage increases with the cubes of their dimensions while the resistance increases at about their squares.' In other words, if you make a ship twice as long, twice as wide and twice as deep, the displacement is eight times as many tons, but the resistance increases by only four times. This means that the bigger the ship the more economical she should be, and it followed that a steamship could cross directly to New York if she were big enough.

Brunel calculated that a ship of about 1,200 tons would be the most economical, and he persuaded the committee, who gave him the green light to build such a vessel. This was to be the *Great Western*, the biggest ship in the world – 212 feet long and 35 feet wide. She was built of massive oak timbers and heavily reinforced with iron. Her engines, made by Maudslay, Sons & Field, drove huge paddle wheels – but she also had four masts and a full set of sails in order to save coal in a fair wind and presumably to get out of trouble if the coal ran out or the engines broke down. She was launched on 19 July 1837 and crossed the Atlantic for the first time in April 1838, in what became a dramatic race.

A rival company, the British and American Steam Navigation Company, hoped to build an even bigger ship, but she was not going to be finished in time to be the first ship to steam across the Atlantic; so they chartered the 700 ton *Sirius*, which normally sailed between London and Cork, and set off from Cork on 4 April. Every scrap of space below decks was packed with coal, and there were two large heaps of coal on deck as well. Unfortunately the coal ran out, and in order to reach New York she had to burn all the cabin furniture, all the wooden doors, all the spare spars and even one of her masts. The remains of the ship limped home after a crossing of eighteen and a half days. The *Great Western*, having set off from Bristol on 8 April, reached New York a few hours after the *Sirius*, but had taken only fifteen days for the crossing and arrived with 200 tons

of coal left in her bunkers. This was a triumph for Brunel's theory that
the bigger ship would be more economical.

In those days the average crossing by sailing packet took thirty-six days
going west, and twenty-four coming home; the *Great Western* averaged just
under sixteen days going west and fourteen days coming back. Alas, however, in spite of her obvious success, Lardner's gloomy doubts had entered
into the public mind. The share capital for the Great Western Steamship
Company was badly undersubscribed. Brunel had hoped to build a fleet
of sister ships, but he had to shelve that idea, and Samuel Cunard was
able to move in and snaffle the business just a few years later.

Despite the lack of enthusiasm from the subscribers, Brunel was determined to go ahead and build another ship, and partly because there is a
natural limit to the size and strength of timbers – trees do not grow infi-
nitely high – he decided to make his second ship from iron. The hull was
designed and repeatedly redesigned, and eventually riveted together in the
Bristol dock where she lies today. While they built her she was called the
Mammoth – at 320 feet long by 50 feet wide she displaced 3,500 tons, which
made her easily the biggest boat in the world – twice the size of any other.

In his second ship, the *Great Britain*, built of iron, Brunel opted for the newly invented screw propeller instead of paddle wheels. This is a modern replica of his original propeller.

Brunel intended to power this iron ship, the *Great Britain*, with Maudslay engines driving giant paddle wheels, but against his advice the directors chose a new engine designed by Francis Humphreys, and in due course appointed Mr Humphreys Engineer in Charge. Humphreys rapidly discovered that no one in the country could forge the huge 30 inch diameter paddle shaft that would have to run across the ship. Hopefully, he wrote to James Nasmyth at Patricroft near Manchester to ask whether he could help. Nasmyth saw at once that the existing tilt hammers could not do the job, and sat down to sketch a new idea in his scheme book – the steam hammer.

Nasmyth's idea was simple. The hammer would be made of a huge block of iron, but instead of being mounted on the end of a shaft, like a simple hammer, this block would slide up and down between two vertical guide rails. The operator would push it up with a piston, driven by a blast of steam in a cylinder, and when he had it as high as he wanted, he would open the valve to release the steam, and the hammer would drop vertically on to the forging.

He wrote and explained his idea to Humphreys and Brunel, who were enthusiastic about it, but then fate intervened in the shape of the *Archimedes*, the experimental ship fitted with the new-fangled screw propeller (see p. 29). Brunel was instantly intrigued, and rapidly captivated. Here was something new, something better – progress – and Brunel was always a sucker for progress. He jumped at the screw propeller in much the same way that he jumped at the atmospheric propulsion system a few years later (see p. 10). At once he told Humphreys that the *Great Britain* would be driven by a propeller, so would Mr Humphreys please redesign his engine accordingly and inform Mr Nasmyth that his great forging would not be needed.

The strain was too much for Humphreys, who had already suffered a good deal of Brunel's aggressive demands, and he died a few days later of 'brain fever'. Meanwhile Nasmyth sadly put his design aside, only to be astonished some three years later when he visited the Creuzot factory in France, saw some huge forgings there, asked how they had been made and was told they had used his steam hammer. The chief engineer from Creuzot had visited Patricroft while Nasmyth was away, had seen the drawing in his scheme book and realised what a tremendous idea it was, so he built one himself. There followed some argument about who should have the patent rights, but they were resolved in Nasmyth's favour, and the steam hammer became one of the major engineering tools of the Victorian age.

The *Great Britain* being towed from dry dock into the Cumberland Basin at Bristol on 19 July 1843 in the presence of Prince Albert.

Humphreys' engine had a drive shaft running across the ship to power the paddle wheels, so to drive the propeller Brunel simply turned the engine through 90 degrees. The *Great Britain*'s six-bladed propeller was 15 feet in diameter and was to turn at fifty-four revolutions per minute – almost one a second. This posed an extra mechanical problem, since the huge steam engines made only eighteen strokes a minute. Brunel's solution was to drive the propeller shaft by a toothed chain with a ratio of three to one – that is the toothed wheel driving the chain had three times as many teeth as the wheel on the propeller shaft.

When the *Great Britain* finally sailed on 10 December 1844, she was both too long and too wide to fit in the lock between the Cumberland Basin and the River Avon. The length was not too much of a problem; they could wait for the right moment at the top of the spring tide and then open the gates at both ends of the lock. To get over the problem of the width they removed some of the masonry from the edges of the lock – already 45 feet wide – in the hope that the great ship would squeeze through. However, when they towed her out on the morning tide she stuck fast, and they had to tow her back quickly before the water level dropped. All day Claxton and Brunel slaved away removing the walls of the dock, and on the evening tide, in pitch darkness, they managed to haul the vast ship through the gap to the river.

In a sense this narrow escape marked the end of Bristol as a great port. In earlier times smaller ships had been content to sail the 10 miles from the Severn Estuary up the narrow, winding Avon, and work their way into the Cumberland Basin and then into the 'floating harbour' where the water level was – and still is – maintained with gates even at low tide. Certainly Bristol harbour is well protected against storms. However, big ships could dock far more easily at Liverpool, where the huge River Mersey gives plenty of room for manoeuvre. As a result, Liverpool became the biggest port in Britain outside London and was well placed for voyages to North America.

So it was into Liverpool that every sort of cargo came, including bananas, sugar, and frozen lamb from New Zealand. The traders brought tales of riches beyond the seas, and it was from Liverpool that no fewer than five million people emigrated, looking for a better life in the New World. Conversely Britain, the land of the conquerors, attracted immigrants from around the globe, and so Liverpool, the port of entry, became the country's first multicultural melting-pot.

THE STEAM TURBINE

The screw propeller brought about a revolution in sea power in the 1840s. However, technology does not stand still, and before the end of the century the Admiralty had its nose put out of joint yet again, by the advent of the steam turbine. Hero of Alexandria made a toy steam turbine 2,000 years ago, and James Watt thought about making one, but realised that the technology was beyond the materials then available. It couldn't be done, he said, 'without [unless] God makes it possible for things to move 1000

Charles Parsons's boat *Turbinia* proved to be much faster than any ship in the navy.

feet per second'. However, his caution did not prevent John Barber from taking out a somewhat ambitious patent for a gas turbine in 1791.

The challenge was taken up by Charles Parsons, youngest son of the third Earl of Rosse, the man who built the world's largest telescope at Birr Castle in Ireland. Parsons became an engineer and lived near Newcastle in a village called Wylam, where railway engineer George Stephenson had been born. There he started working on steam turbines, hoping to find a way to use the enormous expansive power of steam to create rotational motion directly, rather than having to make a piston go up and down in a cylinder, stopping twice on every stroke, and then convert that to-and-fro motion to movement in a circle.

The basic idea was to let the superheated steam stream out of a nozzle at high pressure, and squirt it straight into a set of fan blades – a bit like a toy windmill in front of hair dryer. He realised that the blades of his turbine would have to turn extremely fast, and that there was so much power in the steam that he would have to extract it in two or three stages. In 1884 Parsons took out a patent in which he mentioned the idea of driving boats with turbines, and he began a long series of experiments. Thirty years later he wrote:

> In mechanical engineering, everything depends upon doing something.
> No machine ever reached moderate perfection by sheer thought …
> It is good to remember the crudeness and hopeless inefficiency of the first
> Parsons turbine. Everything was wrong about it except the idea of multiple
> stages … But it taught the designer more than he would have discovered
> by meditation alone.

In 1894 Parsons built a small but magnificent ship, the *Turbinia*, as a sort of test-bed and demonstration model for marine turbines. She was really not much more than a slimline hull with a big engine: she displaced only 44 tons, and was only a 100 feet long. The stoke hold was so small that when she was running at full speed the stoker had to shovel in anthracite continuously, as fast as he could, until he was exhausted. Yet the *Turbinia* was a stunning success. In 1897 there was a naval review to celebrate Queen Victoria's diamond jubilee; Parsons took *Turbinia* along and created a sensation by breaking ranks and zooming up and down the fleet at enormous speed. While the navy's fastest destroyers could just manage 27 knots, the *Turbinia* could do 34. Suddenly they were all out of date.

Before long steam turbines were driving not only the battleship *Dreadnought* but also the big passenger liners, the *Lusitania*, the *Mauretania*, the *Queen Mary* and the *Queen Elizabeth*, while on land steam turbines still generate most of the electricity we use.

NOT SO FAST!

Before the Victorian era the galloping horse was the fastest method of transport, and people had enjoyed horse racing for hundreds of years – Charles II was a great fan, for example. However, towards the end of the nineteenth century a curious bet was to lead to the galloping action being frozen in mid-stride. The man at the centre of this great event was Eadweard Muybridge.

Edward Muggeridge was born at Kingston-on-Thames in 1820. In due course he changed his name to Eadweard Muybridge – because he thought it sounded grander – emigrated to America and became a photographer in San Francisco. He travelled widely and made a photographic expedition to Alaska in 1868, but his most famous horse-stopping work began in 1872.

There was a long-standing argument about how horses galloped. Some

A set of original Muybridge photographs of a racehorse at speed, showing (frames 3 and 4 in the top row) that all four hoofs are off the ground at one point in the stride.

people thought that at some point during their stride they had all four feet off the ground at the same time. Others asserted that they couldn't possibly do this, since they would clearly fall over. And what about when the horse was only trotting? The former Governor of California and President of the Central Pacific Railroad, Leland Stanford, got involved in this argument and bet a friend a substantial sum of money that the horse did indeed have all four hoofs off the ground at some moment in its stride. But how was he going to prove it? Horses gallop too quickly for the human eye to see the process clearly, so Stanford hired Muybridge to provide direct evidence.

Muybridge began on the racecourse at Sacramento, California, and

photographed a celebrated horse called Occident trotting across in front of his camera. In order to freeze the movement of the horse he used extra-fast wet plates and an ingenious shutter with two blinds that were brought together at great speed with rubber bands. He later moved to Leland Stanford's stud farm at Palo Alto, San Francisco, where he set up a row of cameras along the track, and got a sequence of still pictures. After trying various set-ups he settled on twenty-four cameras about 2 feet apart. As the horse galloped or trotted along, it went through twenty-four trip-wires and so released the shutter of each of the cameras in turn. With so many photographs of the horse during one stride of action, he could be fairly certain of capturing a moment with all four feet off the ground – if there was one. And indeed there was. Muybridge's photographs showed clearly that during each stride the horse does lose contact with the ground altogether, and Stanford won his bet.

However, Muybridge's pictures did more than that, for when viewed in sequence they demonstrated the entire process of galloping, and he later extended this to people – athletes from the San Francisco Olympic Club running, jumping, pole-vaulting and playing cricket. Many of his subjects were men, but there were women too, and he persuaded many of them – of both sexes – to perform naked to give a clearer indication of their movements. The results were remarkable, since for the first time they showed many details of animal motion.

On 13 March 1882 Muybridge gave a lecture at the Royal Institution to an audience that included the Prince and Princess of Wales, the Duke of Edinburgh, a variety of royalty and professors, and even the Poet Laureate, Alfred Tennyson. Muybridge's pictures attracted awed admiration from dozens of newspapers and journals. The *Photographic News* said that 'throughout his lecture he was welcomed by a warmth that was as hearty as it was spontaneous. Mr Muybridge wisely left his wonderful pictures to speak for him, instead of making the occasion the subject of a long oration.' He displayed his pictures on the 'zoopraxiscope' that he had invented – a complicated projector system with twin glass discs. The *Illustrated London News* described it as 'A Magic Lantern run Mad (with method in the madness)'. The *Call* said: 'Nothing was wanting but the clatter of hoofs upon the turf and an occasional breath of steam to make the spectator believe he had before him the flesh and blood steeds.' People were astounded that the way horses actually moved was completely different to the way they had traditionally been painted. So Muybridge almost invented cinema; he certainly proved it was possible to make 'moving' pictures by projecting still photographs of moving objects.

During their stay in California Muybridge's wife Flora had an affair with a drama critic called Major Harry Larkyns, a noted charmer, adventurer and con-man. Flora became infatuated and, eventually, pregnant. Muybridge told Larkyns to leave his wife alone, but the liaison continued, and eventually Muybridge tracked Larkyns down at a party. When he met Larkyns at the door, he said: 'Good evening, Major. My name is Muybridge. Here is the answer to the message you sent my wife.' He drew a pistol, shot him dead and turned himself in to the partygoers inside, apologising for the disturbance. In February 1875 he was tried for murder, and amazingly was acquitted; his lawyers pleaded justifiable homicide and insanity produced by mental anguish.

The Victorians invented a succession of simple mechanical devices to show several pictures in rapid succession and so give the illusion of continuous movement. This is a praxinoscope, with the pictures of Zamora in action (see opposite) pasted round the outside and reflected in the mirrors mounted on the central drum. If you spin the drum and look in the mirrors, you see the horse apparently galloping from left to right.

Muybridge Revisited

We decided to recreate Muybridge's classic experiment, to find out whether we came to the same conclusion. At the Metropolitan Mounted Police Training Establishment in Surrey instruc-

tor Vicky Lane generously volunteered to help, with her handsome and wonderfully trained horse Zamora (17.1 hands).

Perry Lewis and Robert Kemp-Smith from Olympus mounted twelve cameras 21 inches (53 cm) apart, the centres of the lenses 8 inches (20 cm) off the ground, pointing directly across the track. These were Olympus E100RS digital cameras, lenses set to a focal length equivalent to about 60 mm for a 35

mm camera, and a shutter speed of 1/650th second at f2.8. The horse was dark, and we hung up a white background for maximum contrast. Across the track we stretched twelve threads of black cotton, which passed through eyes and down to a plastic coffee stirrer. As Zamora galloped into each thread, it jerked out the plastic stirrer from the modified remote control to close a circuit and fire the shutter. Thus the horse took her own photograph twelve times in succession as she galloped along the track. The idea was that those twelve instants would include every part of a single stride, and therefore one of them should capture the moment – if there is one – when all four hoofs are off the ground.

Tests showed that even a human being running through could hardly feel the cotton threads, which simply broke and fell away; there was no danger of the horse becoming frightened or tangled up. A few trials with one camera showed that we needed to position each camera about 2 metres further down the track than its thread, to compensate for the mechanical delay as the cotton tautened, stretched and yanked the plastic stirrer.

On the day we actually did four runs, under slightly varying weather conditions, and with small adjustments to the exposure and the alignment of the cameras. All four were successful, and the last gave the clearest result. You can see the entire stride by flipping the pages, and the critical picture on camera 3 shows all four hoofs perhaps 9 or 10 inches (25 cm) off the ground; the grass is about about 5 inches (12 cm) long.

Watching Zamora carefully, I found the action was so fast that I could not see with my naked eye whether all four hoofs were off the ground together, but the photograph proves that they were; Muybridge was right. What's more, both Zamora and Vicky seemed to enjoy the experience of flying!

See for yourself whether Zamora really did have all four hoofs off the ground in mid-gallop: go to page 79 and flick backwards to see the horse galloping!

CHAPTER TWO

PLAYING GOD

THE EARLY VICTORIAN approach to life was guided by the idea that God had created the world and had then placed mankind in charge of it – to rule over the beasts of its fields and to take benefit from its natural resources. However, people interested in science some-times seemed to be trying to upset this cosy view by interfering in matters that others felt should have been left to God. For example, the opening of Chapter XVIII of a translation of Gaston Tissandier's 1880s book *Popular Scientific Recreations* says: 'We now come to a most mysterious servant of mankind, as mysterious as any Djinn of romance; viz, Electricity.' The writer Arthur C. Clarke once suggested that any sufficiently advanced technology is indistinguishable from magic. Throughout the Victorian era electricity flickered continually between the scientific and the magical.

An illustration from Mary Shelley's Frankenstein.

We live in a world dominated by science and technology, but for the Victorians most of what we take for granted today was new, exciting, some-times even frightening. At the beginning of Victoria's reign electricity was magical, disease an invisible force and death the hand of God heralding the afterlife. But change was afoot: the power of invisible forces was being explored, a modern understanding of disease was developing and the Bible was being challenged by geology. Out of all this emerged the modern scien-tist, rather like Prometheus who stole fire from the gods. To some the scien-tists seemed to be meddling with nature – even playing god.

THE DANGEROUS ELECTRIC FLUID

During the Middle Ages many people thought that lightning was a mani-festation of the wrath of God. When thunderstorms came, they did their best to avert the danger by ringing the church bells, but unfortunately the church was often the tallest building in the area; as a result many churches were struck by lightning and bell-ringers killed.

The American diplomat and scientist Benjamin Franklin was one of the first to undertake serious scientific investigations of the mysterious electricity, and indeed to debunk a little of the mystery and bring this force literally down to earth. In his most famous experiment, in Philadelphia in June 1752, he flew a kite into a thundercloud, and taking care to keep himself well insulated and away from the ground, he was able to draw sparks from a metal key attached to the kite string. The kite string was wet and so conducted electricity from the charged thundercloud down the string and on to the key, which then discharged to earth with a series of sparks. But he was certainly dicing with death: Professor Georg Richmann of St Petersburg was killed trying a similar experiment on 6 August 1753.

Franklin wrote that during thunderstorms trees, spires and chimneys would 'draw the electrical fire' and therefore, when caught in a thunderstorm, you should never shelter under a tree. Wondering how the damage caused by lightning strokes could be avoided, he wrote in his notebook: 'The electric fluid is attracted by points – We do not know whether this property is in lightning … Let the experiment be made.' So he devised a piece of apparatus to test the idea of using points to discharge thunderclouds, and showed that it worked.

In 1754 he proposed that buildings should be protected by sharpened upright rods of iron, gilded to prevent rusting, fixed on the highest parts of edifices and run down into the ground, in order to 'draw the electrical fire silently out of a cloud before it became nigh enough to strike'. In other words, he invented the lightning conductor, and the first lightning conductor in England was installed on St Paul's Cathedral – a neat example of scientific experiment and advanced technology coming to the aid of religion. In practice, as he discovered later, lightning conductors have two functions: first they 'disarm' passing clouds by discharging them, and second if there is a lightning stroke they carry the current safely to the ground.

When natural philosophers began to investigate this dangerous electricity, and even deliberately make some of it themselves, they were often accused of playing God, seeking to take control of what many saw as divine power. Against this background in 1818 Mary Shelley wrote her famous horror novel *Frankenstein, or the Modern Prometheus*, in which the hero, a medical student, uses electricity to animate a lifeless creature.

Until the end of the eighteenth century the investigators had only static electricity to work with, but in 1799 the Italian physicist Alessandro Volta discovered that he could generate electricity by holding together two different metals, such as copper and zinc, which is the basis of battery operation. Volta's invention of the battery utterly changed the course of history, because scientists could then make an electric current when and where they wanted, and no longer had to rely on the instantaneous spark and capricious behaviour of static electricity.

Volta wrote about his discovery to Joseph Banks, President of the Royal Society, and the news spread rapidly through the scientific community. Humphry Davy heard it in Bristol and immediately built a battery of his own. Later, at the Royal Institution, he invented the science of electrochemistry and in 1807 discovered the new elements sodium and potassium. Although he wrote a staid account of this in the scientific literature, his assistant revealed that when Davy saw the first silvery globules of pure metal he shouted with joy and danced around the room, and it was several minutes before he could regain his composure enough to continue the experiment.

On 4 September 1821, also at the Royal Institution, Michael Faraday made the world's first electric motor. It was only a toy, and not until William Sturgeon improved it some years later could it be put to work. However, by 1837 electricity was no longer entirely magical; it was being tamed and used – in the telegraph, in clocks, in motors and towards the end of the century in light bulbs and in medicine, for electric shocks were found to be capable of reviving people after cardiac arrest. In 1871 a German scientist called Steiner revived an apparently dead patient by passing a weak electrical current directly through his heart.

To some extent this particular discovery was unfortunate, since many people saw no difference between this advanced technology and magic, and believed that electricity could do anything. Medical quacks claimed their black boxes with fancy names and electrical wires sprouting from them could cure – at a price – everything from ingrowing toenails to a broken heart. In other words, during Victoria's reign electricity came of age; from the crackling magic chimera of static electricity it turned into the reliable scientific power of current electricity that lit the houses and drove the machines of industry. Faraday's early experiments with motors and with the induction coil led by the 1890s to the generation of vast quantities of electricity by steam turbines (see p. 39).

Engineer James Wimshurst was one of many who remained fascinated by static electricity. During the 1880s he built more than ninety different machines to generate static electricity, of which the most successful has become famous and is to this day called the

Electric corsets were typical of a range of dubious Victorian gadgets. Unscrupulous entrepreneurs cashed in on the general belief that electricity had magical health-giving powers.

Wimshurst machine. It has two large glass discs mounted close to one another on the same shaft – like a pair of giant plates drying in a rack. Turning a handle makes them spin in opposite directions, and a cunning arrangement of brass points and brushes induces and then separates electrical charge, which is usually allowed to accumulate in a pair of 'Leyden jars' or capacitors. When the charge has built up, the machine discharges by sparking between two brass balls. To make a spark one centimetre long in dry air takes about 30,000 volts, and I have seen a Wimshurst machine generating sparks more than three centimetres long, which must have been close to 100,000 volts. High voltages like this were used to power early x-ray tubes.

The Wimshurst machine can generate 100,000 volts of static electricity.

Despite all this progress, however, the myths did not go away. One of the enthusiastic electrical investigators was Andrew Crosse (1784–1855), who lived at Fyne Court, tucked away in the Quantock Hills near Bridgwater in Somerset. He strung a mile and a quarter of copper wire between poles and trees in his garden; there is still a high pole 50 feet up a huge oak tree. This wire acted as a giant lightning conductor; the current was carried through a heavy brass connector into his laboratory in the music room, and during thundery weather he could apparently get twenty discharges a minute, which lit up the five large windows of his laboratory and produced continuous reports like cannon. When the atmospheric conditions were less favourable, he used a huge machine to make thousands of volts of static electricity, although the Wimshurst machine had not then been invented.

The neighbours were understandably a bit nervous of these devilish displays, but because he was the squire they accepted it, and indeed he probably gave some respectability to electrical experiments. He gave a few lectures, and there is a possibility that Mary Shelley

went to one of his lectures in London. He investigated the effects of electricity on everything he could think of, and was highly respected until he
made a surprising observation.

He had been passing a current for fifteen days through a solution of
powdered flint in acid, and when he came to examine the solution he
noticed not the crystals he was hoping for but what seemed to be minute
creatures. Close examination showed they were mites called 'acari', and
he was puzzled about how they had got there. Unfortunately the local
press heard about this, and under the headline 'Extraordinary
Experiment' reported that he had made life with electricity. They even
called him 'The man who was Frankenstein', which made him briefly
famous but damaged his reputation beyond repair. Crosse never claimed
he had created life; indeed, he vigorously denied it. Once the story was in
the press, however, the damage was done.

Apart from electricity, other branches of science also caught the public
imagination. Psychologists were talking of the split personality, and taking
this literally, R.L. Stevenson came up in 1886 with the classic story of *The
Strange Case of Dr Jekyll and Mr Hyde*, concerning the benevolent Henry
Jekyll who made a new drug that changed him into a murderous fiend he
called Edward Hyde. Abraham Stoker was an Irish civil servant who in

1879 wrote a book on *The Duties of Clerks of Petty Sessions in Ireland*, which disappeared without trace. He became a theatre manager, went for a holiday to Whitby in north Yorkshire and wrote another book, called *Dracula* (1897), an amazing gothic horror story about vampires that has been a best-seller ever since. Bram Stoker may have been inspired by the idea of blood transfusion, although he claimed that the idea for the story came to him in a nightmare following a dinner of dressed crab.

Frankenstein, Dr Jekyll and Mr Hyde, The Invisible Man and *Dracula* were all massively popular books that held the Victorians gripped. They all featured a new breed of hero, the scientist struggling with forces beyond his control, and they all implicitly posed a difficult question: were these people merely studying the natural world or were they trying to manipulate nature? In other words, were the scientists playing God?

Electricity and bloody gore were not the only scientific novelties to upset the Victorian equanimity. In some ways more disturbing was the developing argument between science and religion. This had been rumbling for some time, because it was no longer possible for anyone who believed in science to believe also in the literal truth of the Bible.

FOSSILS

Orthodox religious doctrine was challenged well before the Victorian era by fossils found in rocks – 'curiosities', as they were called. They looked like shells and the remains of dead animals and plants, but there were several uncomfortable problems. How had they become embedded in rocks? Why were some fossils that looked like fish and other sea creatures found high up in mountains? And even worse, why did some of them seem to have come from animals that no longer existed? God was supposed to have created the earth and its inhabitants in seven days, and nothing was supposed to have changed since the Creation; so where had these curiosities come from? One dubious answer was that God, while creating the earth, had also created all the fossils in the rocks in order to test the faith of mankind – but this really seemed to be stretching credibility to the limit. There had to be a simpler explanation.

Lyme Regis in Dorset is rich fossil country; the cliffs on both sides of the town are continually being eroded, and many of the rocks that tumble on to the beach contain fossils. The most famous fossil finder in Lyme was Mary Anning, the daughter of the village carpen-

ter. According to legend she was a dull child until at the age of eighteen months she was taken to a fair by three women, who ignored Franklin's advice and sheltered under a tree during a thunderstorm. The tree was struck by lightning, and all three women were killed, but little Mary emerged bright and intelligent – a story almost like *Frankenstein*. She became brilliantly skilful not only at finding fossils in the rocks but also at 'preparing' them – chipping away the rock while leaving the fossilised bones intact – and reconstructing the original animal. When she was eleven she and her brother found what she at first thought was a crocodile in the cliff; it turned out to be the best specimen of an icthyosaurus ever discovered and is still on display at the Natural History Museum in London. Later she found the world's first plesiosaur and the first pterodactyl.

With expert help from Colin Dawes, even I can find a range of fossils on the beach at Lyme Regis.

EVOLUTION AND REVOLUTION

In 1821 William Buckland, the first Professor of Geology at Oxford, found an astonishing collection of bones in the mud on the floor of a cave at Kirkdale in north Yorkshire. There were bones of rabbits and other small animals, bones of giant deer, elephants and rhinos, but above all bones of 300 individual hyaenas. The mud on the floor of the cave had clearly been left there by the biblical flood, he thought, but how had all the bones got in?

Some said the animals were so frightened by the rising floodwater that they ran into the cave to hide, but it seems unlikely that rabbits would choose to shelter in the same cave as 300 hyaenas. Furthermore, the only entrance to the cave is about 2 feet high – quite a squeeze for a Victorian professor – and even the most frightened elephant would have some trouble getting in. Dismissing several more equally unlikely theories, Buckland asserted that the cave had been a hyaena den for dozens of generations, and the bones in the cave were the remains of the food that these carnivores had dragged back home over hundreds of years.

This was deeply upsetting, not only because it suggested that Yorkshire had once had a tropical climate, but even worse that there had been many generations of life before the flood, contrary to the genealogy spelled out in the Bible. The Dean of York thundered: 'If Buckland be right, Moses must be wrong!'

In the 1820s many geologists were catastrophists: they thought that great mountains and plunging canyons had been formed in sudden catastrophic events, probably sent by God. However, Charles Lyell pulled the plug on that idea with his splendid book, *Principles of Geology, being an attempt to explain the former changes of the Earth's surface, by references to causes now in operation* (1830–33). Lyell visited Niagara Falls, duly admired the wonderful sight and noted that the falls had receded 50 yards in the preceding forty years, or in other words the gorge was being extended by rather more than a yard a year. Supposing that this had been going on steadily at the same rate, he calculated that the river could have carved out the entire 7-mile-long Niagara gorge in 10,000 years. Likewise he went to Sicily to see the vast sprawling bulk of Mount Etna, and again calculated that it need not have been formed by a catastrophe, but simply by continual eruptions over many thousands of years. This suggested that God-sent catastrophes were not needed to explain the major features of the earth, which could be accounted for by natural processes such as erosion and eruption, continuing for many thousands of years.

In the 1650s Archbishop James Ussher of Armagh had calculated from the biblical genealogies that the earth was created in 4004 BC, and many theologians still believed this to be true, but Buckland's and Lyell's conclusions made nonsense of Ussher's date. The geologists seemed to be driving a wedge between science and the church. In 1851 the critic John Ruskin wrote in a letter: 'My faith, which was never strong, is being beaten to gold leaf … If only those Geologists would let me alone I could do very well, but those dreadful Hammers! I hear the clink of them at the end of every cadence of the Bible verses.'

The first volume of Lyell's book was published just in time for a young naturalist called Charles Darwin to take a copy with him on a long sea voyage. Robert Fitzroy had become master of the survey ship HMS *Beagle* when Captain Pringle Stokes, depressed after struggling with terrible weather near Tierra del Fuego, had shot himself. The Admiralty surprised many people when they promoted Fitzroy; he was only twenty-three and had limited experience. A small, dark man, he turned out to be a good sailor and navigator but a difficult companion: arrogant, irascible and moody.

Given orders to go back and continue the survey of

The *Beagle* on her way round the world. Darwin was astonished by the variety of plants and animals in South America.

South America, he decided he should take a companion – a well-bred gentleman with whom he could dine and make conversation during the long evenings. Thinking that a naturalist might have the right sort of disposition and would have plenty of opportunity for observation, he made enquiries, and John Stevens Henslow at Cambridge recommended Darwin.

Charles Darwin had two famous grandfathers: Erasmus Darwin, physician, poet, inventor; and Josiah Wedgwood the potter. Both were active members of the Lunar Society of Birmingham. Charles's father Robert Darwin, 'the largest man I ever knew', was also a doctor, and hoping that Charles too would join the medical profession, he sent him to study medicine at Edinburgh University. Unfortunately Charles could not stand the sight of blood, so instead he went to Cambridge to study theology with the aim of becoming a vicar. However, he found he was much more interested in beetles than in God, and when the invitation from Fitzroy came, he jumped at it. Had he known how difficult Fitzroy could be and that the voyage was to last five years, he might not have been so keen.

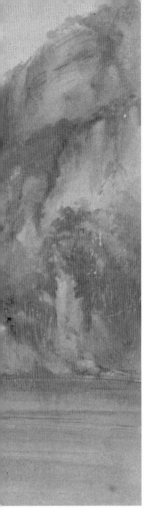

The voyage of the *Beagle* changed Darwin's life completely. He was stunned even by the wonderful variety of plankton in the Atlantic, and then even more so by the exuberance of life in South America. He could not help wondering why there so many different kinds of animals and plants, and where they all came from. Lyell's book helped him to understand how some of the major geological features had come about; could processes that were still going on also affect flora and fauna?

The climax of the voyage came towards the end, when they sailed 500 miles west of Ecuador into the Pacific to the isolated group of Galapagos Islands. These volcanic peaks poking out of the Pacific offered yet more extraordinary varieties of terrain, animals and plants. Darwin wrote in his book *Journal of Researches…* (1839): 'From the regular form of the many craters, they gave to the country an artificial appearance, which vividly reminded me of those parts of Staffordshire, where the great iron foundries are most numerous.'

Crabs and iguanas sweltered in the sun. Giant tortoises with curious patterns on their shells lumbered about, munching prickly pears. The prisoners in exile on Charles Island told Darwin that they could tell simply from looking at these huge beasts which island they had come from, and this was a splendid clue towards the solution to Darwin's problem. Unfortunately, however, he was by then so fed up with the voyage and with Fitzroy that he paid no attention. Merely noting that the turtles made excellent soup, he allowed all the shells to be thrown overboard, thus almost certainly discarding vital evidence in the theory of evolution.

He did shoot a few birds, but failed to label them properly and slung the corpses into one bag to be sorted out later. From the Galapagos they sailed across the Pacific and around the world, and in due course returned to England. Darwin had already become quite well known as a result of the papers he had sent back to Henslow, and he found the scientific community eager to hear what he had to say. He sent off his birds to a well-known ornithologist, John Gould, and Gould alerted the world to the importance of the birds. He wrote excitedly to Darwin, asking for details of which birds had come from which island – but Darwin could not remember and had to go back to Fitzroy and some of the others to discover the details. In the end Gould said that they had shot in the Galapagos thirteen separate species of finches, forming an entirely new group.

The implications of this observation were startling. Because the islands are so far from the mainland, it

seemed likely that they had at some much earlier time been populated by just a few finches. These had bred and spread over the islands, which offered a surprising variety of habitats. An island with masses of insects would favour finches with small pointed beaks, good for tweaking insects out of the grass, whereas an island with plenty of small nuts would favour finches with tough parrot-like beaks capable of cracking nuts. The favoured birds in any particular environment would do better, get fat and strong, and have more babies. And crucially their babies would be more likely to have the same sort of beaks as their parents. Over thousands of generations such variations in beak structure would become steadily more pronounced, until each separated group of finches had actually become a new species. This was a striking example of the survival of the fittest – which was the essence of Darwin's argument about evolution by means of natural selection, described by some as the best idea that anyone ever had.

The actual finches shot by Charles Darwin on the Galapagos Islands.

This idea was what excited Gould, and his enthusiasm got the story into the newspapers. Darwin was more cautious and did not rush into print. Indeed, he sat and thought about his ideas for twenty-five years, gathering more evidence from pigeons, dogs and cattle, before he finally wrote it all up, stung into action by his friend and colleague Alfred Russel Wallace. Darwin's great book *On the Origin of Species by means of Natural Selection* was finally published on 22 November 1859. The publishers, John Murray, even more cautious than the author, printed 1,250 copies, which sold out on the first day.

Darwin's *Origin of Species* shocked the world. Even though scientists had been thinking along evolutionary lines for some time, the idea that evolution was a normal and natural process was dynamite. For one thing it implied that human beings were not special creatures created in God's image and ordained by God to be in charge of the rest of the animals, but had evolved along with other apes, from some common ancestor. In other words, people were just a group of apes that had got lucky. Perhaps even worse, it implied that God was not necessary and that the world had not been created – complete with palm trees waving and lions roaring – in seven days, as laid down in the Bible, but had gradually developed from a more primitive state over millions of years.

Great controversy followed and continues to this day. The most celebrated public debate took place at the 1860 meeting of the British Association for the Advancement of Science in Oxford. In front of an audience of a thousand people Samuel Wilberforce, the Bishop of Oxford, known to the gutter press as 'Soapy Sam' because of his smooth tongue, turned to T.H. Huxley, a staunch Darwin supporter, and asked rather arrogantly whether Huxley was descended from an ape on his grandfather's or his grandmother's side. Huxley retorted that, if the question was would he rather have an ape for a grandfather or a talented man who used his skills to pour scorn on scientific debate, he unhesitatingly avowed his preference for the ape.

Scientists now accept that Darwin was generally right about evolution and have gone on to apply the ideas in other fields. One current theory, for example, is that human culture came about and is still evolving through units of information called 'memes', which are passed on from person to person by imitation. Memes include songs, catch phrases, recipes, fashions and other aspects of culture that animals do not have. Of all the information that pours into our heads every day we remember only a tiny fraction, and the memes we retain are the fittest – the ones that survive. This is why a really catchy tune can stick in your head for hours, and why we remember good stories.

Charles Darwin, photographed by Julia Margaret Cameron.

CHOLERA AND TYPHOID

Death was a frequent occurrence in most Victorian families, which were very large, but in towns in Britain there was a high infant mortality rate when Victoria came to the throne. Babies and toddlers died from typhoid, typhus, cholera, dysentery or just diarrhoea. Cholera was especially frightening, because it was a new disease. The first case, apparently brought from India, appeared in Newcastle in 1831, and there were major outbreaks in 1849 and 1854. Early symptoms were uncontrollable diarrhoea, fever and vomiting, and most victims died within a few

'At the court of King Cholera': the disease flourished in the unsanitary cities, and many thousands died.

days, some even within twenty-four hours. There was no cure, and no real treatment.

We know now that cholera and these other diseases are transmitted by contamination of the water supply. Before 1850, however, there was no clear idea of how they spread. The tropical disease malaria was thought to come from 'bad air' – which is what malaria means – and similarly, cholera and so on were thought to be carried by 'miasmas' – gaseous exhalations, or terrible smells. They thought an awful stink like rotting flesh or human sewage was a warning of the deadly miasma; anyone who breathed it in was in danger. This view had hardly changed since Roman times; the Romans built efficient sewers (*cloacae*) to get rid of the smell of the sewage, rather than because they thought it unhealthy. Unfortunately this 'miasmic theory' of disease turned out to be a powerful but unhelpful meme; because so many people were convinced by it they overlooked the real culprit.

Gradually, however, medicine was becoming more scientific, and in the middle of the nineteenth century various doctors began to apply scientific principles to finding out where diseases came from. William Budd caught typhoid while serving in the navy on a hospital ship moored at Greenwich. He recovered, but when typhoid came in 1839 to his home farming community of North Tawton in Devon he was particularly interested in how it spread. He knew everyone in the village, and therefore found it easy to chat to all those who were afflicted about exactly which members of the family had showed the earliest symptoms and when they had started. Most people got their drinking water from the little streams flowing through the village, and he noticed that those who lived downstream showed symptoms a few days after their neighbours upstream. He came to the conclusion that whatever caused the disease must be carried by contaminated drinking water.

Meanwhile in London John Snow had been working independently on cholera, and had reached similar conclusions. After studying an outbreak in 1849, which claimed 55,000 lives, Snow published a report on 'The mode of communication of cholera', in which he suggested that, because the first symptoms were diarrhoea, vomiting and fever, the infectious agent, whatever it was, must surely be swallowed. He did not believe it could be carried through the air, partly because he had personally attended dozens of patients without catching the disease himself. Also, if you breathed in the infectious agent it should affect the lungs. However, no one took much notice of his report because the miasma theory was so widely believed, but when cholera came again in 1854 Snow took dramatic action.

There was a virulent outbreak in the district of Soho, almost on the doorstep of Snow's practice in Frith Street. The rate of infection was frightening: 56 cases were reported on the night of 31 August, 143 on 1 September and 116 on 2 September. Within a couple of weeks 500 people had died in an area not much bigger than a football field. The spread was so rapid that Snow was convinced that drinking water was to blame; how else could the poison affect so many people in just a few days? He went to the Registrar of Deaths, got details of all those reported dead and marked their positions on a map of the area, which showed that they were clustered round Broad Street (now Broadwick Street), where there was a popular water pump.

Only five people died in the workhouse in Poland Street, a hundred yards from the pump, but the workhouse had its own well, and they did not use water from the Broad Street pump. None of the seventy workers in the Broad Street Brewery died, but they drank only beer. The clinching cases were those of two ladies who died in Hampstead,

5 miles away. Snow discovered that one of them was particularly fond of the taste of the water from the Broad Street pump, and every day had sent a carriage specially to fetch a large bottle of it. She and her niece both drank the water on the Thursday and the Friday, and on the Saturday they died.

Convinced, Snow persuaded the authorities to remove the handle from the pump so that no one else could drink the water, and the outbreak rapidly died out, although by then Soho was almost deserted, for most of the healthy inhabitants had fled. The well was 28 feet deep, and it turned out that a leaking sewer was contaminating it 22 feet down. The epidemic was probably started by one infected person who happened to be using that sewer. As the outbreak continued the water became steadily more infected.

Snow did not know about the leaking sewer, and he certainly did not know about the organism that caused cholera – but he did not need to. He was able to work out how the disease spread by sheer logic and detective work, and he and Budd could be said to have founded the science of epidemiology, which is still one of the most powerful tools in the continuing fight against disease.

SCIENTIFIC SURGERY

Before the middle of the nineteenth century there were no anaesthetics. At least, Humphry Davy had discovered the anaesthetic effect of nitrous oxide, or 'laughing gas', way back in 1799, and had proposed that it should be used in surgery, but no one listened to him. To some extent this was because of a general belief that surgery and pain were inseparable. Even during childbirth the men who controlled the medical profession decreed that pain was normal and even necessary.

Without anaesthetics, the most important factor for the surgeon was speed. His assistants could hold down a patient in agony for only a few minutes, during which the entire operation must be complete. Suppose the victim had slipped under a carriage and suffered a smashed lower leg. This was essentially impossible to repair, and would generally become infected, gangrenous and swollen with pus, which meant that the leg would have to be amputated either mid-thigh, or if the patient was lucky, just below the knee.

Imagine the scene in the old operating theatre in St Thomas's Hospital in London, which was a wooden garret above the old church and well out of earshot of the wards, so that the patient's screams would not terrify the others. The rails are packed with 150 doctors and medical students, all hoping to learn the skills of the experienced surgeon, all leaning over and jostling for a better view of the table, almost like a stage; this really was an operating *theatre*. The surgeon comes in, wearing a filthy frock coat, and puts on an equally filthy apron to protect himself from the mess of pus and blood. He will not wash his hands until later.

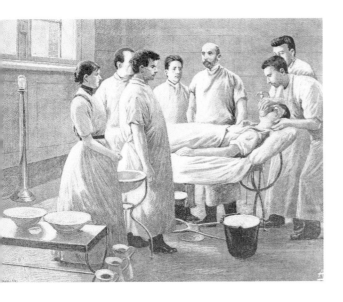

He takes a large straight-bladed knife from the box of instruments, turns to the audience and commands: 'Time me, gentlemen, please!' Speed was of the essence; this was surgery by the clock.

The patient, nerves steadied with a dose of laudanum or more commonly brandy, lies on the bare operating table and is held down by several strong young medical students, one of whom presses down hard on the femoral artery at the top of the thigh to prevent major bleeding. The surgeon performs the *tour de maître* – a single cut all the way round the thigh, down to the bone. Grabbing his saw he saws through the femur, and if all

The arrival of anaesthetics meant that the patient no longer needed to be held down during surgery.

goes well the leg is off in thirty seconds. The leg and a pint or two of blood goes into the sawdust-filled box on the floor, the arteries are tied off and then the surgeon washes his hands. Some patients died of shock, some from loss of blood and others from infection of the new wound. The mortality rate from this type of operation was about 30 per cent.

Luckily for patients, an American dentist called William Morton experimented with ether in 1846 and found that by making his patient unconscious he could work much more easily. On 21 November that year Oliver Wendell Holmes, Professor of Anatomy at Harvard, proposed that this new process should be called 'anaesthesia'. When the news spread to England the keen young Dr John Snow took up the practice with enthusiasm, and later made it fashionable by persuading Queen Victoria to have chloroform during the births of Prince Leopold in 1853 and Princess Beatrice in 1857. This royal approval ensured the general acceptance of anaesthetics, and surgery was transformed.

Although ether was the first anaesthetic to be used, it

was tricky to administer and is dangerously flammable, which made it highly risky in gas-lit rooms when the patient's lungs were full of an explosive mixture of ether and air. Chloroform was both easier to use and also non-flammable, and therefore became the favourite, although it too could be dangerous; a patient called John Shorter went to St Thomas's to have a toenail extracted and died from an overdose of chloroform.

The difference produced by anaesthetics was tremendous. Because the patient was unconscious, and not screaming and writhing, speed was no longer the primary consideration. The surgeon could work slowly and carefully, avoiding unnecessary damage to the tissues and giving a much better chance of recovery. There was time to clean up the wound and carefully tie or sew up the blood vessels, and the patient was less likely to die from blood loss or from shock. Because speed was no longer of the essence, surgeons could now invade the body, removing gallstones and inflamed appendices, which before then had been almost impossible. Finally, because the patient no longer needed to be held down, medical students could be chosen for their brains rather than their brawn!

Joseph Lister, antiseptic pioneer.

The result was that surgeons gradually changed from butchers to scientists. The mortality rate did not immediately plummet, because they became more adventurous and tried ever more difficult procedures; in just the same way the death rate in the mines did not fall when the miners' safety lamp was introduced in 1815, because armed with their new lamps the miners went into ever more dangerous mines in pursuit of the coal. Furthermore the risk of infection after surgery remained as high as ever.

However, a second great step forward in surgical practice was eventually to make a profound difference. This was antiseptic surgery, introduced in Glasgow in 1867 by Joseph Lister. A little boy had broken his arm, and Lister knew that infection would probably set in. He had heard that carbolic acid was effective at cleaning drains, and he wondered if it would clean wounds too. He carefully cleaned the boys arm with carbolic acid and the arm did not get infected. Because it prevented a wound from becoming septic, the carbolic acid was called antiseptic.

Lister went on to design a carbolic acid spray so that even the air in the

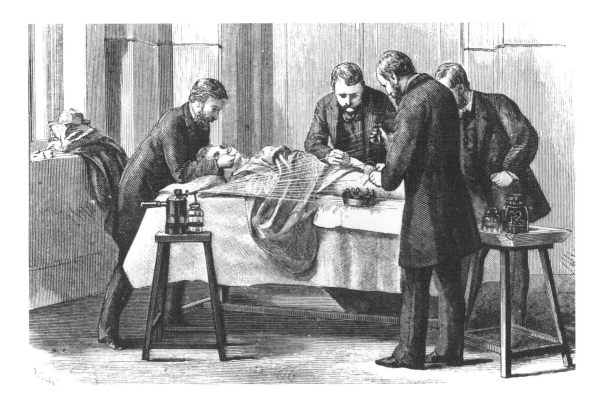

Lister's antiseptic spray in action.

operating theatre would become saturated with antiseptic. This must have been unpleasant for everyone – patient, surgeon and all – because carbolic acid, now more commonly called phenol, not only has a powerful smell but also is a mildly caustic material that quickly roughens the skin. However, Lister realised that the germs that carry infection might lurk not merely in the air but also on the instruments and on the clothes and the skin of the patient and the surgeon. Instruments were quickly redesigned, and instead of having wooden handles they were made entirely of metal so that they could be sterilised. Surgical gloves were introduced in 1876, and surgeons began to wash their hands before the operation instead of afterwards. The progress from antiseptic surgery to the aseptic surgery of today was slow but steady, and the mortality rate at last came down.

RESURRECTION MEN

Throughout the Victorian period doctors became more scientific and their social status improved. As the population grew, so did the demand for doctors, and the medical schools expanded. But this raised a problem;

the only way these students could find out about how the body worked was by anatomy lessons; they had to watch corpses being cut up to expose the tissues and organs. The supply of an ever-increasing number of corpses to the medical schools became a dark and unpleasant business.

The bodies of criminals, who died in gaol, and of paupers, who died in the poor house, were generally available for dissection, but there were never enough of them, and unscrupulous entrepreneurs began to rob graves to find fresh bodies. They were sometimes called 'resurrection men', and apparently sold the bodies by length – so much a foot, with a special price for 'smalls', i.e. children. The Victorians were appalled at this dark trade and built high railings around their graveyards, locked the gates at night and paid night watchmen to guard their dear departed, but still the grave-robbing went on.

As the city population grew, the numbers of deaths increased as well, and the city graveyards filled up at an ever-increasing rate. In one London parish 180,000 bodies were said to be crammed into a churchyard of only three-quarters of an acre, which suggests that a hundred bodies must have been occupying each 6 foot by 3 foot plot! What it meant in practice was that thousands of bodies were exhumed and the bones disposed of to make room for new occupants, and the average body was buried for only six months or so before being dug up again.

In 1852 a new Act of Parliament came into force; large cemeteries were created well outside the city, and the bodies were shipped out to lie in peace beyond the suburbs. There was even a dedicated platform at Waterloo Station in London, which was known as 'Necropolis Station'; the entrance to the platform is still visible on Westminster Bridge Road. The trains went direct to a special station that opens directly on to the 30 acre Brookwood Cemetery, where, incidentally, Dr Robert Knox, accomplice of body-snatchers Burke and Hare, was buried. William Burke and William Hare, Irish labourers on the Union Canal near Edinburgh, heard about the shortage of bodies for anatomy classes in the city and began robbing graves. Then, tired of digging, they started killing people instead and were not caught until they had committed sixteen murders.

Perhaps even more terrifying than grave-robbing was the possibility of being buried alive. Stories were told of coffins that had been found with scratch-marks on the underside of the lid, showing that the unfortunate 'corpse' had woken up too late and had been buried while merely unconscious. I suspect these stories may have been made up by enterprising inventors, who produced dozens of devices to avoid such a catastrophe. In

1843 Christian Eisenbrandt patented a spring-loaded coffin lid, so that if you woke up in the mortuary or even on your way to the graveyard, you could open it at the touch of a button and let everyone know that you were still alive.

C.H. Nicolle was worried that you would be short of air in a sealed coffin, and patented a spring-loaded hammer that, when activated from inside the coffin, would smash a glass panel in the lid, and so let air in. There was a slight drawback in that the window was over the face of the occupant, and so pressing the trigger would give you a faceful of broken glass, followed by a hammer-blow between the eyes.

Adembert Kwiatkowski invented a spring-loaded flag that would wave above the grave to show there was someone alive below, but perhaps the most comprehensive patent, taken out by Walter McKnight of Buffalo, New York, described an all-electric device for 'indicating the awakening of persons buried alive'. This was designed to work even if you woke up 6 feet underground, for a large tube extended to the surface and carried the wires to ring an electric bell above ground.

SURVIVAL AFTER DEATH?

In 1848 a curious thing happened in Hydesville, a small town in upstate New York. In a modest wooden house three young sisters called Katie, Leah and Margaretta Fox said they were in contact with the spirit of a dead person – apparently a tinker who was buried beneath the house. Their parents were intrigued and, when they asked questions of the 'spirit', received answers in the form of raps or knocking sounds. Using simple codes like one rap for yes and two for no, they quickly established what seemed to be interaction with a soul beyond the grave.

Word spread to friends and neighbours, and before long the Fox sisters were giving public demonstrations. Soon others too were establishing such spiritual communication. The craze spread across North America and then came to England, and the drawing rooms of London began to echo with raps, taps and eerie sounds. Professional mediums appeared, who would (for a price) attempt to contact your dear departed in the spirit world. At a typical seance half a dozen people would sit in a circle, perhaps at a table, and the lights would be turned low. The medium would go into a trance, frequently groaning and calling for her 'spirit guide' who often seemed to be a Red Indian or an ancient Egyptian.

Although most mediums were women, their guides were often male and seemed to speak, through their mediums, in deep throaty voices.

Mental mediums confined themselves to speaking to the spirits, but physical mediums produced apparently impossible phenomena: icy breezes would suddenly blow in the faces of the sitters, trumpets would float around the room, touch the sitters on the heads and speak of their own accord. Sometimes objects appeared on the table – arrowheads or semi-precious stones, which the medium would explain were 'apports, precipitated from the fourth dimension'. Some mediums produced yards of 'ectoplasm' from their mouths, noses or other orifices; it looked and felt like muslin, but apparently came from the world beyond the grave.

Two of the most famous mediums were Eusapia Palladino and D.D. Home. Palladino was an illiterate Italian woman who was said to be able to levitate herself and large pieces of furniture, and materialise extra limbs during seances – while sitters firmly held both hands she would still manage to wave a couple of arms about.

Eusapia Palladino (centre) with two sitters and what looks like a levitating table.

Daniel Dunglas Home (pronounced 'Hume') was unusual in that he normally worked in well-lit rooms, rather than in dim light or total darkness. In 1894 Sir William Crookes, pioneer of the cathode ray tube and early experimenter in atomic physics, reported of Home: 'I once saw him go to a bright wood fire, and, taking a large piece of red-hot charcoal, put it in the hollow of one hand, and covering it with the other hand, blew into the extempore furnace till the coal was white hot and the flames licked round his fingers.' Home was said to levitate miscellaneous objects – at one session an accordion played by itself as it floated through the air. His most spectacular feat, however, was to levitate himself; on one occasion he apparently floated out of one window of the room and in at the next. Crookes postulated that Home generated a 'psychic force' that made such phenomena possible, but never managed to explain how it fitted in with the normal laws of physics.

Some mediums were frauds – quite a number confessed that they fooled the sitters with simple conjuring tricks and conned money from gullible grievers. Photography in one way made things worse, because photographs of 'spirits' (usually double exposures) were used to 'prove' the existence of the afterlife. However, as scientists brought to the seances better photographic technology – flashguns and infrared film – so the physical mediumship curiously faded from sight. And in 1888 the Fox sisters publicly admitted that they had never believed in the spirits; they had learned to click their joints and make curious rapping noises, using the furniture to amplify them, and had made up all the communication with the 'spirits' just because they were bored. But by then it was too late; the genie was out of the bottle, and millions of people believed in the reality of the spirit world – indeed, millions of people still do.

One of the most common phenomena in the early days was table-tipping. The participants would sit round a table, resting their fingertips lightly on the edge, and wait, in the near-darkness, for something to happen. Suddenly the table would shudder, and the sitters would often jump with surprise and then settle again, arms out, fingers lightly on the table. Then came a real movement, small but sure, and another lurch. Gradually the table's movements became more and more dramatic, until it seemed to dance around the room – and yet afterwards all the sitters would swear that they had not pushed it at all; indeed, just to follow its movements had taken all their energy.

There is no doubt that tables do move in these conditions; in the twentieth century the extraordinary phenomenon was often captured on film. But what could be going on? Why should the spirits want to move the table, and how could they do it.

In the early days many scientists were highly sceptical of the whole gamut of 'spirit' performances, and one man who investigated things seriously was Michael Faraday. He devised two clever experiments to establish whether the table was really moving on its own. First he asked a group of sitters to put their fingers not directly on the table but on a special mat he had made and placed in front of each of them. This mat was actually a sandwich of three layers of card separated by not-quite-dry glue. At the first movement of table or hand the layers would slide and the glue would set. If the table were to move first, then

A time exposure of Lord Combermere's study, taken while his funeral was in progress. In the chair on the left you can see the face and right hand of a shadowy figure. Is this a servant who came into the room and sat briefly in the chair before he noticed the camera and moved away? Or could it be the ghost of Lord Combermere revisiting his favourite room?

the hands should lag behind and the top layer would slide towards the sitter, whereas if the hands moved first the top layer would slide away. Faraday showed to his satisfaction that the sitters were definitely pushing the table, even though they resolutely denied it. He then set up a simple pointer system – a similar mat of two cards without glue but with a long straw pointer sticking up. If the sitter's hands moved across the table the pointer would swing in a movement obvious to all. Under these conditions the table did not move at all.

Faraday's explanation, all written up in *The Times* and later in the magazine the *Athenaeum*, was that after sitting for perhaps half an hour with their arms outstretched the sitters would get very tired, and their arms would be subject to unconscious muscular twitches. Even though they would not be aware of it, they would stir the table. The other sitters, attempting to leave it alone or to keep it still, would actually push it back the other way, and so the table would begin to rock. As far as Faraday was concerned, unconscious muscular action explained everything; there was no need to invoke any supernatural agency.

Nevertheless, many sitters in seances of all kinds were utterly convinced that they had indeed made contact with the spirits of their loved ones; they recognised their voices and turns of phrase, and if the medium was an artist they often recognised the portraits the medium sketched. They must have been greatly comforted in their grief by these brief contacts, but spiritualism had a more fundamental and general effect. To some extent the advance of science was undermining religion. Geologists and evolutionists were saying that the world had not been created in 4004 BC, as the Bible suggests. This wonderful possibility of contacting the spirits restored some faith in the non-material world.

Some scientists, uncomfortable with the anti-spiritual Darwinian view of things, turned their skills and their instruments on spiritualism, in the hope that science could prove that there really was life after death and that heaven was worth striving for. Sir William Crookes photographed mediums in action. Sir Oliver Lodge, the man who sent the first ever message by radio, before Marconi came to England, was a staunch supporter, and part of the headquarters building of the Spiritualist Association of Great Britain is dedicated to him.

In 1882 a group of academics, including three from Trinity College Cambridge, formed the Society for Psychical Research, or SPR, which ever since has been one of the world's best-known organisations for the investigation of paranormal phenomena. One of their first actions was to

conduct a colossal survey, the Census of Hallucinations, in which they asked people whether they had ever come across a ghost. Their actual question was: 'Have you ever, when believing yourself to be completely awake, had a vivid impression of seeing or being touched by a living being or touched by a living being or an inanimate object, or of hearing a voice, which impression, so far as you could discover, was not due to any external cause?' An astonishing 17,000 people replied, of whom some 10 per cent said they had, and this percentage hasn't changed much over the years; modern surveys commonly find that around one person in ten claims to have seen a ghost. One of the surprising things about that original census was that it produced 830 first-hand accounts of realistic human apparitions, of whom only one fifth were of dead people; by far the majority were ghosts of people who were still alive.

CHAPTER THREE

THE CONQUERORS

Edward Whymper, conqueror of the Matterhorn.

IN 1860 A TWENTY-YEAR-OLD wood engraver called Edward Whymper was sent out to the Alps to make sketches for a book by William Longman, who was a publisher and President of the Alpine Club. Whymper became fascinated by climbing and decided to go for the Matterhorn (14,700 feet), which was thought to be unclimbable. Seven times he tried and failed, but he finally reached the summit in July 1865, the first person to make it, although there was a terrible accident on the way down and four of the team died. He had a rival in the famous Irish scientist John Tyndall, who had joined the Royal Institution in 1854 and had also become fascinated by the mountains. Tyndall attempted to climb the Matterhorn in 1860, succeeded in 1868 and was the first to climb the Weisshorn (14,800 feet) in 1861. Being a keen scientist, Tyndall calculated that the energy he would need to climb the Matterhorn was the same as the energy contained in a ham sandwich, and the story goes that a ham sandwich was all he took to eat! Whether or not this is true, the fact remains that two of the most inaccessible peaks in the Alps were first climbed, not by the Swiss, the French or the Italians, but by the British, the Victorians, the 'conquerors'.

By the 1850s the Victorians were sure that Britain was at the centre of the world. They had an unfailing belief in progress and in the power of human endeavour and new technology. With their mastery of iron, their steam engines and sheer brain-power they took over the high seas and international trade, and they could build almost anything they wanted, from washing machines to swing bridges for railways. Meanwhile chemistry was producing new synthetic dyes, so their clothes were becoming bright and beautiful. Their doctors were ever more scientific and would soon discover the cures for many diseases. They achieved extraordinary feats of engineering, exploration and control, and they truly believed in themselves as the conquerors.

THE GREAT EXHIBITION OF THE INDUSTRY OF ALL NATIONS

The most spectacular display of Victorian pride and progress was the Great Exhibition of 1851, housed in the amazing iron-and-glass building that the new magazine *Punch* had, in a moment of misplaced sarcasm, called the 'Crystal Palace'. In six months more than six million visitors – a quarter of the entire population – travelled to London's Hyde Park to see it. They paid their shilling – after the first three weeks, when the entrance fee was higher to give preference to the upper classes – and spent all day walking around the breathtaking exhibits.

The idea of holding such an exhibition was not new; the Society of Arts had organised them each year since 1845, and they had been successful, attracting steadily increasing interest in manufacturing, science and the arts. However, the idea of holding a vast international event was novel, and the prime mover, Henry Cole, was skilful in persuading the right people to get involved. He approached Prince Albert early on, and the Queen's young consort was keen but, because he was not immensely popular with the people, was cautious about joining the planners too soon. However, once the event gained the support of elder statesman Sir Robert Peel in the summer of 1849, Albert publicly declared his enthusiasm, and Cole astutely encouraged people to believe that the whole thing had been the Prince's idea in the first place. This royal patronage must have provided a tremendous boost to both exhibitors and potential visitors.

The doors opened on 1 May 1851, which turned out to be a wonderful sunny spring day after weeks of rain. Crowds began to gather by six in the morning, and before the doors opened at nine some 300,000 people had come to see the spectacle. When the Queen and Prince Albert walked in at noon, bands played *Rule Britannia* and then the national anthem. After a long speech by Albert, he and the Queen went walking through the exhibition – the first-ever royal walkabout, which concluded a fine opening to the event. The newspapers, previously sceptical of the entire enterprise, turned in their tracks and devoted supplements and even whole editions to describing and praising the exhibition. *The Times* said it had 'an effect so grand and yet so natural that it hardly seemed to be put together by design, or to be the work of human artificers', while *Punch* declared: 'Prince Albert has done a grand service to humanity, and earned imperishable fame for himself.'

The Queen loved it. She wrote about the opening ceremony in her journal:

> The tremendous cheering, the joy expressed in every face, the vastness of the building, with all its decoration and exhibits … and my beloved husband, the creator of this peace festival 'uniting the industry and art of all nations upon earth', all this was indeed moving, and a day to live forever. God bless my dearest Albert, and my dear country, which has shown itself so great today.

Furthermore, her enthusiasm lasted, for she visited the exhibition whenever she could – at least five times in May alone – and spent some fifty hours there. She was not alone. People came from far and wide, whole villages arriving on excursions organised by their vicars. Special trains, some organised by Thomas Cook, brought six or seven hundred people at a time from towns across the country. There were hundreds of visitors from France and Germany and America, which was probably the first time that foreign tourists had ever been invited into the country. There was plenty to see – an eclectic mixture of political propaganda, public education, religious celebration, industrial salesmanship and art gallery.

There were sculptures, fountains, and the massive Koh-i-Noor diamond lit from below by gaslight and locked inside an immense iron cage. From Canada there were timber, minerals and a Montreal fire engine. An eighty-bladed penknife from Sheffield and a sixteen-ton chunk of Welsh coal rubbed shoulders with a huge model of the Liverpool docks and a bust of Shakespeare made of the new Portland cement. Arts and sciences were curiously blended: the French photographic display had artistic daguerreotypes, while the English one presented photography as a scientific curiosity.

Rhubarb champagne was exhibited, along with condensed milk, and food preserved in tins. There were French furniture, Swiss watches and exotic artefacts from China, Turkey, Spain, Portugal, Tuscany and India – even a stuffed elephant, which must have been extraordinary to people who had not even seen pictures of such a thing. This had been hastily brought in to hold up an elegantly decorated howdah (elephant rider's seat) from India and unfortunately was actually an African elephant, on loan from a museum in Bury St Edmunds. There were fine silks, lace, embroidery, velvet and grisly medical exhibits of glass eyes, false noses, artificial arms, and a patent fulcrum and chair for extracting teeth.

The American display was relatively simple, because of the difficulty in bringing huge machines across the Atlantic, and the Queen remarked on her first visit that it was 'not very interesting'. What she missed were the

The Inauguration of the Great Exhibition, 1 May 1851, 1852 (detail), by David Roberts.

labour-saving devices from the land where the space was vast and labour scarce: sewing machines, typewriters and mechanical harvesters; rubber goods made by Goodyear; and, perhaps even more fundamental to future industrial development, machines made from interchangeable parts, in particular Colt revolvers. According to *The Times*, 'Great Britain has received more useful ideas and more ingenious inventions from the United States, through the Exhibition, than from all other sources'.

But above all the visitors marvelled at the machines brought from all over Britain – Nasmyth's steam hammer (see p. 37), a GWR locomotive from Swindon, washing machines, steam ploughs, reaping machines, cotton-spinning machines, working looms including a Jacquard loom, and especially De La Rue's envelope-folding machine which, according to the *Illustrated London News*, 'followed several actual movements of the human form divine' and, controlled only by two children, turned out sixty envelopes a minute.

Mercifully, the visitors were reasonably well catered for. They could not buy alcohol, thanks to temperance pressure and fears of drunkenness, but during the six months they bought in the refreshment courts two million buns and a million bottles of soda water, lemonade and ginger beer, not to mention savoury cakes, pies, ham, potted meat and a phenomenal amount of jelly, which had just become popular with the working classes. There were plenty of complaints about the food, but at least there was something to eat and drink. Furthermore, both men and women could relieve themselves, in public lavatories. The flamboyant plumber George Jennings had designed and installed these, and then announced his intention of charging each user a penny to use a cubicle. Many of the organisers were outraged, and protested that the public would be coming to see the exhibition, not to go to the lavatory. In the event 827,280 people chose to 'spend a penny' – which is probably where that expression comes from – and no doubt at least as many men used the urinals, which were free.

The Great Exhibition was a people's exhibition; it was funded by private subscription rather than with public money, and the exhibits were chosen by the people, not by some government committee – in stark contrast to the Millennium Dome 150 years later. Furthermore, the Great Exhibition was enormously successful; not only did six million people visit in six months, but it made a profit of £185,437. This was used, along with an equal amount of public money, to buy 70 acres of land south of Hyde Park, on which were eventually built the Science Museum, the Natural History Museum, the Victoria and Albert Museum, the Royal

The Indian howdah at the Great Exhibition, perched on the back of an African elephant from Bury St Edmunds.

Geographical Society, the Albert Hall and Imperial College of Science and Technology.

The Great Exhibition attracted rivers of poetry, some even from Tennyson, the Poet Laureate, but the feeling of philanthropic satisfaction seems to me to be well summed up in these lines:

> For it is a glorious teaching,
> Albert, thou hast taught mankind,
> Greatly to perfection reaching,
> And enlarging heart and mind;
> Stirring us, and stirring others
> Thus to do the best we can
> And with all the zeal of brothers
> Help the Family of Man!

This is the ending of Martin Tupper's *Hymn of the Crystal Palace*, which underlines the fact that the greatest exhibit of the whole of the Great Exhibition was its extraordinary home, the Crystal Palace.

JOSEPH PAXTON AND THE CRYSTAL PALACE

Joseph Paxton had a miserable childhood, and after being beaten and starved as a teenager he ran away to become a gardener, eventually getting a job as foreman at the Chiswick Gardens Arboretum. The pay was poor, and he had decided to go and seek a more prosperous life in the new world of America when one day he opened the door to the Duke of Devonshire, who owned the place, and his life changed in an instant.

Paxton was only twenty-three at the time, but the Duke was so impressed by his manly bearing and his love of gardening that he hired him as chief gardener at his country house, Chatsworth in Derbyshire, one of the great stately homes of England. Paxton was nervous and excited, and could not sleep the night before he went there, so he arrived at 4.30 in the morning. He climbed over the wall, walked around the estate, inspected the water works, met the labourers, had breakfast with the housekeeper and fell instantly in love with her niece Sarah Brown – they later married and had a baby – and all this was before 9 o'clock in the morning!

The Duke gave Paxton a free hand, and he developed a superb horticultural display, starting with huge fountains, one of them twice the height of Nelson's Column. He built an arboretum, a conservatory 300 feet long and an extraordinary greenhouse. In 1837 a traveller had brought back a new giant lily from Guyana, which the experts at Kew Gardens had been unable to grow. Paxton got hold of a seed and designed a specially heated pool, with water wheels to keep the water flowing, in which the lily flourished. Within three months it had huge flowers and eleven leaves, each 5 foot across. He named it *Victoria regia* and presented a bud to the Queen. Today it is called *Victoria cruziana*, and you can see the giant leaves at Kew Garden in June.

This lily was far too big to grow in normal conservatories, and he had to work out a way of designing bigger spaces. In due course, after some trial and error, he built a modular structure made of wood and glass, with gutters outside to collect rainwater and inside to collect condensation, and hollow pillars to hold up the roof and carry the water away. But the most radical and brilliant idea behind the final design was that all the pieces were prefabricated and simply assembled in place. He designed the machines to make the parts, which were manufactured in vast numbers.

For the building to hold the Great Exhibition the Building Committee invited designs from the public, received 245 entries and then rejected

Joseph Paxton stood his young daughter on one of the giant lily leaves in 1849 to demonstrate its strength, but he may have placed a box underneath to make sure the stunt worked! Amazingly the huge plant grows from seed every year.

every single one. Their own design looked rather like a railway station – hardly surprising, since the Building Committee included Robert Stephenson and Isambard Kingdom Brunel – and was clearly not for a temporary structure, as planned. Moreover, it was so ugly that it provoked a public outcry when it was published. At this point Paxton stepped in and submitted a design based on his novel greenhouse; it was to be a building made entirely of iron and glass, constructed in modular sections and bolted together on site. The Building Committee and the public quickly took up the plan, and on 26 September 1850 the contractors Fox Henderson, who had much experience in building shipyard roofs, put the first pillar in place.

The final building was a symbolic 1851 feet long and covered 26 acres; there would have been space for twelve football pitches on the ground floor alone. St Paul's Cathedral had taken thirty years to build; the Crystal Palace, six times the size, was put together in nine months. This was a remarkable example of innovative structural engineering, and a demonstration of the Victorian belief that they could conquer any problem by

Rebuilding a Corner of the Crystal Palace

Following the original structure of 1851, can Dominic Grosvenor recreate a corner of the Crystal Palace and erect it on site? He runs a small iron foundry in Wolverhampton, so in principle producing the cast-iron columns should not be too difficult, but they were enormous – 18 feet long – and as far as he knows no one has tried to make anything this size since Victorian times. He was able to match the original design precisely by using parts of old columns, and making a sand mould directly from them.

The glass posed an additional problem. Today it would be made by the Pilkington float-glass process, pouring molten glass on to a lake of molten tin, so that as the glass cools and hardens both top and bottom surfaces are completely smooth and flat. However, in 1851 this process was a hundred years in the future, so the Victorians had to make their panes by blowing glass into cylinders and then opening them out. Unfortunately English glass-blowers could not manage the huge panes, 49 by 10 inches, and Fox Henderson had to get the 300,000 panes from French and Belgian glass-blowers. This turns out still to be the case, and historical-glazing expert Ben Sinclair had to go to France for the huge panes of hand-made glass.

On the great day, almost exactly 150 years after the opening of the Great Exhibition, Dominic set off long before dawn with his heavy load, more than a ton and a half of cast ironwork, all painted white and shrink-wrapped for protection. On site at the south-east corner of the original building, almost opposite the back of the Horseguards' barracks, he parked his lorry and supervised the unloading. Ten strong men were just able to carry each 300-kilogram column across the riding path to the grass where they were needed. The first column was carefully lifted with a small hand-powered crane until the bottom end could be manoeuvred into place on the steel base, and bolted down.

Once all three columns were up, the connecting pieces at the top were hoisted up and bolted into place. This was one of the trickiest parts of the whole operation, and eight or ten men were needed to rock the columns gently and twist the various pieces in order to line up the holes for

the bolts. But then, suddenly, the majestic shape became clear – the elegance of the arches, and the way that they framed the view.

Finally three sample panes of handmade glass were slid into the slots already cut in the wooden frames, and the effect was almost magical. The handmade cylinder glass has a slightly rippled appearance and seems to shimmer as the light reflects from its surface with delicate irregularity. At the same time, looking through it, the fresh young leaves seemed to flutter on the trees as their positions appeared to change with the slight distortions in the glass.

What a superb achievement! With a little help from his friends, Dominic managed to give us a glimpse of what it must have been like, 150 years ago, to look at that wonderful building, the Crystal Palace.

Champagne to celebrate the rebuilding of one arch of the Crystal Palace in Hyde Park.

ingenuity and scale. The building was over 100 feet high, and was actually built round and over two large elm trees, which flourished inside. There is a story that once the building had enclosed the trees a flock of sparrows moved in, delighted to be out of the rain. The question of how to get rid of them was tricky; clearly shooting was out of the question because of the glass. The Queen is supposed to have asked the canny old Duke of Wellington, whose eighty-second birthday coincided with the exhibition's opening day. He replied, 'Well, Ma'am, you could try a sparrowhawk.'

The Crystal Palace cost only £80,000, which was remarkably cheap, and when the Great Exhibition was over, it was taken down again and re-erected at Sydenham, where it remained until destroyed by fire in 1936. Paxton's idea was quickly taken up and echoed in many other exhibition buildings, and also in more mundane structures – you can see the hollow iron columns and the glass-and-iron construction at Paddington Station today.

INTREPID EXPLORERS

Driven by their belief in their own omnipotence, the Victorians were determined to expand their trade routes across the globe, to open up the dark continent of Africa, to help guide poor uneducated peoples to Christianity and morality, to conquer the world and to build an Empire. They knew they were right, and they were fearless in their pursuit of progress.

Armed with pith helmets, compasses, bibles and guns, they were confident of coping with crocodiles, lions and hostile natives, but a more serious problem was posed by mosquitoes. Most Britons who ventured into the tropics seemed to catch malaria, and even if the disease did not kill them, it came back again and again and was utterly debilitating; West Africa was known as the white man's graveyard. The only antidote was quinine, found in the bark of a South American tree called cinchona (pronounced sinka-una), but the Spanish had control of most of the supplies, and the British could not get hold of it.

Then along came Richard Spruce, from Ganthorpe in Yorkshire, a botanist who was the opposite of a rolling stone, for he gathered mosses in profusion, first in the Yorkshire Dales and then in the Pyrenees. In 1849 he went off to South America, met Alfred Russel Wallace there, and after some extraordinary journeys collecting 7,000 new species of plants, he was commissioned by the India Office in 1859 to get hold of cinchona. On the western slopes of Chimborazo he collected 600 plants and 100,000 seeds, which were transported to India – that is, into British territory. Ever since then, quinine has been available to British travellers.

Later, at the very end of Victoria's reign, the exact mode of transmission of malaria was worked out by another Briton, Ronald Ross, working in India. Basically the anopheles mosquito bites a malaria victim, picks up the deadly plasmodium in the blood that it sucks up, and then infects someone else a few days later, when the plasmodium has developed. Ross was so excited at his discovery that he wrote a poem about it:

> This day relenting God
> Hath placed within my hand
> A wondrous thing; and God
> Be praised. At His command,
> Seeking His secret deeds
> With tears and toiling breath,
> I find thy cunning seeds,
> O million-murdering Death.
> I know this little thing
> A myriad men will save.
> O Death, where is thy sting,
> Thy victory, O Grave!

When he heard about the brand-new Nobel Prizes, Ross wrote to the committee in Sweden and asked whether he could have one. The slightly acid reply said that they would decide who should receive these great honours – and then in the following year, 1902, Ross was indeed awarded the Nobel Prize for Medicine.

Even though we now know precisely how it is transmitted, malaria remains a deadly disease; thousands die from it every year, and travellers to the tropics should always take quinine for protection. Tonic water contains a small quantity of quinine, and the rubber planters of Malaya sometimes claimed that they drank vast quantities of gin and tonic in order to ward off malaria…

Of all the Victorian explorers, perhaps the most famous was David Livingstone, a medical doctor and scientist who spent thirty years discovering and recording the geography of Africa. Born in Lanarkshire, he became a cotton spinner, studied with William Thomson (later Lord Kelvin) at Glasgow University and was ordained as a missionary. He wanted to go to China, but was unable to because of the opium wars, so

instead he set off in 1840 for southern Africa. In 1843 he was attacked and mauled by a wounded lion, and his left arm was permanently damaged, but he did not allow that to slow him down, and continued travelling, exploring, treating the sick and preaching to the heathen. In November 1855 he discovered a 350-foot-high waterfall on the Zambesi River and named it the Victoria Falls, after the Queen. The following year he returned to Britain, was greeted as a hero, met Prince Albert, was elected a fellow of the Royal Society and presented with a gold medal at a special meeting of the Royal Geographical Society.

He went back to Africa in 1858 and stayed for a turbulent six years, during which time he became terribly ill and his wife died of fever. He returned to Africa for the third time in 1866, disappeared into the interior and again travelled incessantly, suffering the most dreadful hardships. After

nothing had been heard of him for several years, the proprietor of the *New York Herald* sent a journalist called Henry Morton Stanley to look for him, alive or dead. Stanley, too, had a tough time for several months but at the end of October 1871 finally discovered Livingstone at Ujiji on the shore of Lake Tanganyika. The story goes that when they first met, Stanley presented himself in the most polite Victorian manner, raised his hat and said 'Dr Livingstone, I presume?'

They travelled together for four months, and although Stanley tried to persuade him to return to England, Livingstone was obsessed with finding the source of the Nile; so Stanley came home alone and Livingstone carried on travelling, perpetually struggling through swamps, continually ill and incessantly bitten by mosquitoes, spiders and ants. He died on 30 April 1873; his roughly embalmed body was encased in a cylinder of bark and brought back to England by his African friends to be buried in Westminster Abbey. The President of the Royal Geographical Society

David Livingstone discovered and named
the Victoria Falls (painted left in 1862),
on the Zambesi River, and was later
himself discovered by American journalist
Henry Morton Stanley (above).

wrote of him: 'the work of his life will surely be held up in ages to come as one of singular nobleness of design and of unflinching energy and self-sacrifice in execution … I never met a man who fulfilled more completely my idea of a perfect Christian gentleman.'

Perhaps less of a gentleman and more of an entrepreneur was Cecil Rhodes, described in the *Dictionary of National Biography* as 'imperialist and benefactor'. He was born in 1853 in Bishop's Stortford and was sent to southern Africa for his health when he was seventeen. When diamonds were discovered at Kimberley, he became a diamond prospector and acquired a large fortune in a couple of years, before returning to study at Oxford. For eight years he oscillated between Oxford and Africa, getting a degree and setting up the De Beers Mining Company. He went into politics and eventually became Prime Minister of Cape Colony. His ambition was to bring the whole of Africa, from Cairo to the Cape, into the British Empire, and by a series of manoeuvres he managed to colour pink a good deal of the map of southern Africa. A whole country, Rhodesia, was named after him, and in his will he left enough money to fund about 200 Rhodes scholarships for overseas students to go to Oxford University.

Mary Kingsley, another fearless traveller, was born in London and remained quietly at home until her parents died in the early 1890s. On holiday she met several ship's captains who had travelled to West Africa, and she decided she had to go there to study religious practices and natural history. She made tremendous river journeys through regions where no European had ever been seen, let alone a woman on her own, and climbed the 13,400 foot Mount Cameroon. On her third trip, in 1899, she went to Cape Town to work as a nurse, looking after the wounded and the prisoners in the Boer War, and there at the age of thirty-eight she caught typhoid and died.

Livingstone's and Kingsley's travels and travails in Africa must rank as some of the most uncomfortable and heroic journeys of all time, but for sheer romance and mystery my prize goes to John Franklin, who spent much of his life searching for the Northwest Passage to India. If you look at a globe you will see that the voyage from England to India going all the way round Africa is very long; it would be much shorter if ships could sail north-west, past Greenland and over the shoulder of North America – provided there is a passage through the ice. Many sailors set out to look for such a Northwest Passage, but none more tenaciously than John Franklin.

John Franklin takes *Erebus* and *Terror* into Arctic waters in search of the north-west passage in 1845.

Born in Spilsby in Lincolnshire, Franklin made three expeditions in search of the Northwest Passage. The first ended quickly in disaster when one of his ships was crushed in the ice, and they had to limp home. For the second he went to Canada and travelled overland, hoping to follow the northern shore and so discover where the passage might be. The weather was terrible, the natives were unfriendly, and in one bleak area marked on their map as 'Barren lands' eleven men died of starvation, and the others actually had to eat their boots to stay alive. After seven years as Lieutenant Governor of van Diemen's Land (now Tasmania), Franklin volunteered to lead yet another expedition. When his interviewer pointed out that he was already sixty years old, Franklin said 'No no, sir – only fifty-nine!'

In 1845 he set sail with two ships, the *Erebus* and the *Terror*, and 138 men. After being sighted on 26 July in Baffin Bay, they were never seen alive again, even though at least forty expeditions were sent out to look for them. Some remains were found, and a note that suggested Franklin had died on 11 June 1847. They were carrying food preserved in tins sealed with lead, and one possibility is that they died from lead poisoning. But the strangest part of the tale is that in 1851 some Italian sailors near Newfoundland said they had seen in the distance two ships, one upright and one on its side, frozen into an iceberg. We shall never know whether they were the *Erebus* and the *Terror*, drifting off to their end in the icy wastes of the North Atlantic.

> In Baffin's Bay, where the whale fishes blow
> The fate of Franklin no one may know.

NAVIGATION

By the middle of the nineteenth century travelling by sea was becoming less of a dangerous adventure – one to be undertaken only by the seriously brave – and more like the tourism of today. In particular the advent of the SS *Great Britain* and other huge iron ships at least gave the appearance of safety – the Victorians seemed to have conquered the waves. Charles Dickens went for a reading tour of America; Tchaikovsky sailed to New York to conduct at the opening of Carnegie Hall; and the *Great Britain* carried the first cricket tour to Australia.

However, life did not always run as smoothly as clockwork. On 22
September 1846 the *Great Britain* set sail from Liverpool with 180 passengers
– the largest number ever to have embarked on a trans-Atlantic voyage –
including 48 little girls from a German dancing troupe. About ten o'clock
that evening, when the captain thought he was near the Isle of Man, the
ship ran aground in Dundrum Bay, about 60 miles further west. No one
was badly hurt, but the great ship was stuck fast, and despite tremendous
efforts remained there for almost a year. The loss of revenue and the cost of
the rescue almost sank the Great Western Steamship Company, which had
to put up both the *Great Western* and the *Great Britain* for sale.

How could Captain Hoskens have been so wrong about where the ship was? It turned out that a lookout had spotted St John's Lighthouse on the Irish coast, but this was not recorded on the admiralty charts, and Hoskens assumed it was Chicken Rock Light on the Calf of Man. The suggestion was also made that the compass may not have been working properly. Compasses depend on the interaction between a magnetised needle and the earth's magnetic field. This works well in wooden ships, but in iron ships the magnetic field is enormously distorted by the iron. Brunel and Hoskens would certainly have realised this, but they may have been unable fully to compensate for it.

The binnacle on the Mersey Ferry.

Compensating for compass deviation on an iron ship was an intriguing problem – one of many technological difficulties that needed a scientific solution – and after baffling many clever men, including the Astronomer Royal, George Airy, it was solved by the great William Thomson, Lord Kelvin. Born in Belfast in 1824, he was Professor of Physics at Glasgow University for fifty-three years from 1846 until 1899, and was one of the greatest scientists of the Victorian age. He found an old Stirling engine in a cupboard, and was so intrigued by it that he worked out some of the basic principles of thermodynamics in order to explain its behaviour. He proposed the absolute scale of temperature, and scientists now measure temperature in 'kelvins'. He developed new methods for transmitting electrical signals along wires, and advised on the laying of the first trans-Atlantic cables. When he was made a peer, he took the title Baron Kelvin of Largs from the river Kelvin that flows through Glasgow University.

He redesigned the mariner's compass and sorted out the problem of compensation for an iron hull, which turned out to be a complicated business. Today, there are main corrector magnets fixed inside the binnacle – the wooden stand that holds the compass 4 feet above the floor. In the middle of the binnacle there also hangs a 'heeling bucket' with further bar magnets whose number and height are adjustable to cope with variation when the ship heels over. Outside, near the top of the binnacle, are two large 'Kelvin spheres' of soft iron (not magnets) whose distances from the binnacle are adjustable, and finally at the back is the brass Flinders bar, with yet more soft iron pieces for fine adjustments. Modern ships have radar, global positioning by satellite, and fixes from radio beacons, but they also have adjustable Victorian-style binnacles, just in case of failure of the electronic navigation aids.

Ideally each time a ship docks at a new port, the captain takes on board a compass adjuster, whose job is to tweak the positions of the magnets and soft iron pieces while the ship is sailing in known directions, so as to bring the compass as nearly as possible into line with reality. Even the Mersey Ferry, which sails to and fro between Liverpool and Birkenhead, has her compass adjusted every year.

WHETHER THE WEATHER BE STORMY...

As more and bigger ships took to the high seas, and increasingly they carried passengers who were not sailors at all, storms became more of a worry. The possibility of shipwreck was all too real. Every year in the early 1850s about a thousand ships were wrecked and a thousand lives lost near the British coast.

All sorts of life-preserving inventions were produced, ranging from the folding lifeboats of Edward Lyon Berthon (see p. 28) to the 'Improved Suit ... for Saving Life in Water' patented by Captain John Benjamin Stoner in 1870. This comprised a rubber suit to be put on over all your normal clothes, plus an outer jacket of cork to keep you warm and floating. There was a hood to cover your head and neck apart from your face, and lead weights attached to your ankles to keep you upright. In addition, you had an floating buoy containing flares, rockets, a flag for attracting attention, paddles to propel you through the water, and a box loaded with drinking water, food, cigars and reading material. I suppose you were meant to have a relaxing read and smoke while waiting to be rescued, although I do not understand how you were supposed to carry all this equipment about with you at all times, in case of shipwreck.

Rather more practical were the Victorian efforts to predict storms, to enable evasive action or other precautions to be taken. At the Great Exhibition Dr George Merryweather proudly displayed his 'tempest prognosticator'. This was an elegant gilded cage some 18 inches across containing twelve glass jars. In each jar was an inch of water and a medicinal leech. In stormy weather leeches, stimulated perhaps by the high electric fields caused by thunderstorms, crawl upwards and so reach the tops of their jars; presumably this is a survival instinct to escape floods. If they try to go any higher, they press on a small piece of whalebone and so activate a trigger, which releases a fine gold chain. This in turn allows a small hammer to fall against the bell at the top of the cage.

Each of the twelve leeches was independent, but together they were expected to provide a statistically reliable warning: when the owner of a tempest prognosticator heard the bell ring he might expect some unsettled weather, but if it rang four or five times in quick succession he could be sure that a storm was imminent. Once triggered, the hammers remained against the bell, so that if they all went off in the night when no one was there to hear them, the first person there in the morning could see the danger at once and raise the alarm.

A modern replica of Dr George Merryweather's gold-plated tempest prognosticator.

Dr Merryweather hoped for government money that would allow him to install his prognosticators at strategic places on the coastline, and therefore build up a national network of storm prediction. Unfortunately his invention, though ingenious, was not given the support he thought it deserved, and in due course it was replaced by a rather more scientific instrument, the barometer.

Barometers had been around for some time – since Torricelli made the first one in the seventeenth century – but they had not been used in a systematic way until Robert Fitzroy (see p. 55), soon to be promoted admiral, became Head of the Meteorological Department of the Board of Trade in 1854. He was all in favour of a national network and began by collecting weather information from ships' captains; he then set up twenty-four observing stations around the country. The most important step was to issue them all with standardised barometers – simple instruments, with instructions on how to use them printed on the cases. Because all the barometers had been standardised at Greenwich, he knew he could rely on the readings. Each day he received weather information from all twenty-four stations and compiled a synopsis in the form of a weather map.

A small memorial on a cliff top in north-west Anglesey records a terrible disaster on 26 October 1859. At three in the morning the sailing ship *Royal Charter* sank in a gale offshore, with the loss of 400 lives and half a million pounds' worth of gold bullion, for the passengers were returning from Australian gold fields. The ship ran on to a lee shore and was only a hundred yards from the beach, but it was said that the passengers were unable to swim because they were weighed down by the gold in their pockets; and there were terrible tales, quite unfounded, of locals stealing the gold.

Fitzroy wrote a report about the disaster and pointed out in words of one syllable that he could have predicted the storm, at least twelve hours in advance, using the information he had gathered. As a result, he was encouraged to issue storm warnings, and he invented a simple display system. If he thought a southerly gale was imminent he arranged for south cones to be displayed in all the ports. Similarly a north cone warned of a northerly gale, and a drum signified generally stormy weather.

But he went further than this and in August 1861 began to predict the weather, which was the first time anyone had seriously tried to do so. From 1862 his weather forecasts were printed in *The Times*. We now know, with the benefit of hindsight, that forecasting the weather is incredibly difficult, partly because of the mathematics of chaos theory, which means that a butterfly flapping its wings in South America may lead to a thunderstorm in Britain a few days later. In those days no one understood, and Fitzroy was ridiculed because he kept getting the forecasts wrong. In 1864 questions were asked in the House of Commons. Even *The Times* said: 'We must … demand to be held free of any responsibility for the too common failures which attend these prognostications. During the last week Nature seems to have taken special pleasure in confounding the conjectures of science.'

Fitzroy was always a difficult and touchy man, not good at taking criticism and subject to fits of depression. He had been relieved of his position as Governor of New Zealand because he had made a mess of diplomatic relations, and this attack on his latest venture was too much. On 30 April 1865 he went into the bathroom, took his razor and cut his own throat.

Though his end was tragic, Fitzroy's initiative in forecasting the weather was an important step towards the conquering of nature's fury, and it would not have been possible without another great technological leap – the electric telegraph. In the early stages Fitzroy had to collect his weather data by post, but as the telegraph spread across the country he

A modern version of Admiral Robert Fitzroy's storm barometer.

was quick to grasp the advantage of instantaneous communication; the telegraph meant that he could compile his weather map within hours of the records being taken.

EARLY TELEGRAPH COMMUNICATION

In the late eighteenth century a brilliant but dilettante Irishman called Richard Lovell Edgeworth devised a mechanical signalling device in order (it is said) to get the racing results from Newmarket before his bookmaker. Unfortunately he was rich enough not to need such a system, and he never bothered to develop it. Perhaps he was too busy with his many other inventions – including steam engines, a turnip-cutting machine, new clocks, a salt dish with an integral spoon, and a close-stool pan – and with his family, for he had four wives, one after the other, and a total of twenty-two children.

Twenty years later in France a clever chap called Claude Chappe invented another mechanical signalling system, which came to be called the *télégraphe* (meaning 'distant writing'), and was essentially like mechanical semaphore. Mounted on a vertical post was a cross-beam that could swivel from vertical through diagonal to horizontal. On each end of the beam was a pointer, which could also swivel. Each position of the beam and the pointers represented one number in a code book, which contained 9,999 words and phrases.

In a demonstration on 12 July 1793 the not-very-exciting message, 'Daunou has arrived here; he announces that the Convention Nationale has just authorised its Committee of General Security to affix its seals to the papers of the representatives of the people', was transmitted 21 miles in eleven minutes. Later Chappe's *télégraphe* was said to be able to transmit orders from Paris to Marseilles in half an hour. One problem was that using this code system every message had to be checked back, since one small error would lead to a totally different message being sent.

For some reason no one worried much about security, and within a month a copy of the code book got into British hands, but they did not pay much attention, until the Admiralty woke up to the fact that long-distance signalling might be useful, and chose a method developed by George Murray, who was awarded £2,000 in 1796. His system was much simpler: an array of six shutters, each of which could be open or closed, represented the letters of the alphabet plus a few common phrases, such as 'Ready to receive' and 'Message ends'. Every morning a time signal was sent from Whitehall to Portsmouth, and apparently covered the 63 miles in forty-five seconds, although real messages travelled at only about six characters a minute. Murray's telegraph lines were laid also from London to Deal, Yarmouth and Plymouth. The French system was used until the 1850s, but the British mechanical telegraph went quickly out of fashion after the patenting of the electric telegraph in 1837.

THE VICTORIAN INTERNET

Once Michael Faraday had made the first electric motor in 1821, people realised that they could use electricity to move things and that by using long wires they could make signals at a distance. Many people tried to develop practical systems, including an American called Samuel Finley Breeze Morse, who took out a US patent for an electric telegraph in 1840 and whose Morse code became the standard method of sending messages in North America.

Meanwhile, on the other side of the Atlantic William Fothergill Cooke abandoned his study of anatomical modelling after seeing a telegraph demonstration in Germany. Cooke rushed back to England and began to construct his own telegraphic apparatus, starting with musical boxes, which he knew all about, but he was no scientist and could not get it to work over any appreciable distance until he teamed up with Charles Wheatstone. Wheatstone, born in Gloucester into a music family, invented the concertina and was fascinated by sending sound along stretched wires. Indeed, he hoped in this way to be able to 'broadcast' concerts and also parliamentary speeches.

Wheatstone was a good scientist, and when he heard about Cooke's work he understood at once how to get the telegraph working. They formed a partnership and patented the electrical telegraph in June 1837 – the very month of Victoria's accession. They rightly guessed that the electric telegraph might be useful for the new railway companies. The telegraph wires could easily be laid beside the railway lines, and messages could be sent from one station to the next or to a signalling point. This would clearly be a good way to control the use of a single railway line; to prevent trains meeting head-on, the signals at both A and B could normally be set to 'wait', and when a train was ready to use the line at A, a signal could be sent to B to switch the signal to 'stop'.

Robert Stephenson's London and Birmingham Railway was the first to try out the telegraph between Euston and Camden, though surprisingly they decided not to install a permanent system. However, Brunel's GWR did take it up, and by 1843 the telegraph extended from Paddington to Slough.

The early five-needle telegraph needed five wires to operate, and these were originally laid in a tube beside the rails, but as the system evolved it eventually came down to a single wire, which was usually slung off the ground between poles. Stringing the telegraph wires alongside the rapidly expanding rail network made it easy to develop a telegraph network, too. By 1857 most of the big towns in Britain were linked, and by 1862 there were 15,000 miles of telegraph wires. The whole network was eventually taken over in 1870 by the General Post Office, which also swallowed up the telephone system that developed in the late 1870s.

Once the wires were in place all sorts of people, apart from the railway companies, realised that they could make use of the telegraph. Large businesses began to build their own local connections and use the existing network to send messages from one branch to another. Private individuals began to send one another telegrams. And above all the telegraph was used to send news. In August 1844 it achieved a wonderful coup by carrying to London the news of the birth of the Queen's second son at Windsor. In 1845 the telegraph itself made news by enabling the capture of a murderer called John Tavell. Disguised as a Quaker, with a beard and distinctive hat, he went to Slough, killed his mistress with cyanide and then ran to the railway station to escape to London. Unfortunately for him, the woman screamed and alerted the neighbours, who saw the 'Quaker' getting on the train. A message was telegraphed to London, warning the police to meet the train and watch out for a 'kwaker' – they were unable to send the letter Q on the primitive five-needle telegraph – and he was duly arrested and convicted.

WILLS'S CIGARETTES.

FIVE-NEEDLE TELEGRAPH INSTRUMENT.

The five-needle telegraph. Two of the needles across the centre of the diamond swing to point to one of the twenty letters in the display.

The Electric Telegraph Company was unusual in championing the employment of women as operators; they did the job better than men.

The rapid early expansion of the telegraph system needed a huge amount of capital, which Cooke and Wheatstone could not raise on their own; the 'railway mania' of 1845 meant that they needed £71,000 to keep up with the demand that year alone. At this point Wheatstone, rather curiously, decided that he did not enjoy the business and sold his shares for some £7,000 at extremely short notice. With the help of various friends, including the engineer George Parker Bidder, Cooke set up the Electric Telegraph Company, which was incorporated early in 1846.

The growth of the telegraph system had an unexpected benefit in the shape of employment for women. The Electric Telegraph Company, commonly called 'The Electric', engaged six female operators in 1850, and the number steadily grew, until by 1870 there were more than 200 female clerks at the central office in London. There was tough competition for these jobs, and an examination to be passed, so getting in was no easy matter, but the company promoted the employment of women. One official later wrote, 'Their dexterity made women good manipulators. The work was sedentary which women bore with patience, unlike their male counterparts. They were better educated and could spell and write better.'

As the telegraph spread across the country, the conquerors wanted more: why not also send messages overseas – or rather under the sea. First the wires had to be insulated, since salt water conducts electricity, and no electrical signal could survive in a wire that made contact with the sea. Luckily there appeared in Britain in the 1840s a new tough white plastic material called gutta-percha, which came from the sap of trees in Malaya, already more or less under British control. Gutta-percha, until recently used to cover golf balls, is like rubber but not springy, and is a good electrical insulator, as Faraday noted in 1848, and far better than the tarred hemp they had used before. In 1850 Jacob and John Watkins Brett ordered 25 miles of copper wire coated with gutta-percha, and laid the first cable from Dover to Calais. It failed rapidly, but they ordered another, this time protected with an outer sheath of iron rope, and laid it the following year. It worked well and proved highly profitable.

Spurred on by this success, others started laying cables all over the place, and set out to cross the Atlantic in 1857. The first two attempts failed, the third lasted only a month, but in 1866 a pair of cables was successfully laid between Britain and America from Brunel's vast ship the *Great Eastern*, chartered by Sir Daniel Gooch, who had been Brunel's engine-builder at Swindon, and went on to send the first ever trans-Atlantic telegraph signal and later to rescue the Great Western Railway from financial disaster.

Laying a cable across the Atlantic was a colossal undertaking. Not only did they need thousands of miles of enormously strong and heavily insulated wire but they had to lower the huge weight of cable into deep,

Unwinding the cable from the hold of the *Great Eastern* while laying it across the Atlantic in 1866.

unknown ocean trenches and avoid breaking it every time the ship lurched in the wind. After one of the cables broke and had to be grappled and hauled to the surface, the sailors found it was encrusted with marine creatures, which was astonishing, since no one had imagined that anything could live under the enormous pressure in the gloomy depths of the oceans. Finally, as if all the mechanical problems were not enough, they had great difficulty in detecting an electrical signal after passage through 3,000 miles of wire. In the early days Cooke was defeated by a few yards. Science had moved on, and passing a signal a few miles was relatively simple, but after 3,000 miles the tiny signal was almost completely lost in the resistance of the wire. They might not have succeeded without con-

Inside the small hut above Porthcurno beach where cables from around the world emerged from the sand. This was the hub of the Victorian internet; the cables in this picture were actually connected directly to Newfoundland, to France, to Spain and to Gibraltar from where they went on to India and Australia.

siderable help and scientific advice from Lord Kelvin, who was intensely interested in such practical problems. He also sorted out the ship's compass (see p. 92) and constructed the first machine to predict the tides, which led to the production of tide tables for ports in Britain and around the world.

By 1875 cables had been laid to India, the Far East, Australia and around the coasts of Africa and South America, most of them controlled by the 'cable king' John Pender. Pender had been a textile merchant in Manchester, but foresaw the tremendous potential of submarine telegraphy and devoted the rest of his life to it. In 1870 he formed the Falmouth Gibraltar Malta Telegraph Company, which gradually expanded and was operating all the way to Australia within a couple of years. He actually laid the cable into the sea not in the busy port of Falmouth but on a quiet sandy beach at Porthcurno, just a few miles from Land's End. Within a few years Porthcurno became the communication gateway to the British Empire.

One immediate result of the cable to the Far East was that the British Empire gained in influence and control – in particular over the gutta forests that supplied the insulation material so necessary for all the cables. More generally, the worldwide communications system enormously consolidated the British dominance of world trade, and the Queen, who had her own telegraph station at Buckingham Palace, could send out an instantaneous personal message to the Empire.

In 1851 Julius Reuter had opened a news agency, developing a network of agents who supplied stories to and from the European continent. At first they mainly used the post, but they quickly adapted to the electric telegraph. News of the fall of Napoleon I in 1815 took two weeks to reach America, but when Napoleon III fell in 1870 the Americans knew about it within a few hours. Reports of Abraham Lincoln's assassination in 1865 took twelve days to reach England, but when President Garfield was shot in 1881 the news was printed in London the following day.

From 1858 Reuters delivered 'electric news' to the London newspapers, and their telegrams were often printed directly, unedited, one above the other, regardless of subject. The editors made lofty statements about their mission – 'to Enlighten, to Civilize, and to Morally Transform the World. These are the grand purposes which Providence has in view in relation to our race,' as one of them put it – but what really interested people was bad news, especially of war. During the Franco-Prussian War of 1870–71 the vivid reports from war correspondent Archibald Forbes trebled the circulation of the *Daily News* from fifty to a hundred and fifty thousand. Incidentally the cleverly named *Daily Telegraph* was started in 1855 and by 1870 had the highest circulation of all the London daily newspapers.

Before the electric telegraph most wars were remote from government control. Army commanders were on their own and autonomous on the battlefield. However, the telegraph changed all that, because war correspondents could reveal what really happened, and reports of triumphs or disasters could appear in newspapers the following day. At the same time the government at home could keep in touch with the action in the field, and assume control when they wanted. The telegraph brought command and control to the hub of the Empire.

George Parker Bidder was born in Moretonhampstead on the edge of Dartmoor and became fascinated by numbers; indeed, he was a wizard at mental arithmetic. His father even exhibited him at fairs as the Calculating Boy. In spite of this he became a fine engineer and had a remarkably clear vision of what the telegraph meant for the future of communications. As early as 1851, at a meeting of the Institution of Civil Engineers, he said that 'the time would come, when individuals would correspond directly with each other … and the most important affairs would be concluded without personal communication and independent of distance … the necessary spread of telegraphic communications was almost too vast to be calmly contemplated.' He really did foresee something like email and the worldwide web.

CHAPTER FOUR

PLEASURE SEEKERS

WHEN THOMAS COOK arranged the world's first publicly advertised excursion train on 5 July 1841, he can't have realised what a precedent he was setting. Today the posters in the windows of the high street travel agents are forever shouting at us to have a week in Ibiza or a month in Bali. His trip was a day's outing from Leicester to Loughborough for a temperance picnic. It cost a shilling, and it was a sell-out; 570 passengers packed the train. For the first time ordinary people were beginning to have money, and they wanted to enjoy themselves. Leisure had arrived for the growing middle class.

To Brighton and back for three and sixpence (17.5p), painted in 1859.

GETTING AWAY FROM IT ALL

The countryside had previously been a dismal, cold, smelly place where people slaved away on the land, earning a pittance by milking cows and herding pigs. Suddenly it became a desirable retreat from the fumes of the city and the tyranny of the mill, and the most desirable retreat of all was Scotland. The royal couple visited Scotland in 1842, 1844 and 1847, and even though the 1847 trip was drenched with continuous rain, they were so delighted by the country that in 1848 the Queen bought Balmoral Castle, without ever having seen it. They rebuilt the castle, acquired more land and decided it was a perfect royal retreat.

She made a point of going there for six weeks every autumn, and expected foreign dignitaries to travel all the way up there to see her. She promoted such things as hunting, shooting, fishing, and especially the highland games, which had before been rare and obscure. With Victoria's approval the highland games became a must for wealthy travellers from Europe, and the royal family has patronised the Braemar games ever since. The grouse-shooting season begins on 12 August each year, and clearly all the important people had to be in Scotland for the 'glorious twelfth'. So Parliament always rose in good time for them to get there,

Dining car on
the Orient Express
in 1884.

and the constitution settled itself around the new royal playground; in effect, Victoria invented Scotland!

The Queen normally travelled there by train, and this helped to promote the idea that trains could be used for leisure, and by the grandest people. There gradually appeared not only first-class carriages but whole luxury trains, designed for comfort and elegance. The most famous was probably the Orient Express, started in 1883 by a wealthy young Belgian banker called Georges Nagelmackers. The train, fitted with sumptuous sleeping and dining cars, ran from Paris to Istanbul, although to begin with the passengers had to cross the Danube by boat and finish the journey from Bulgaria by Black Sea liner. From 1888 the train ran all the way to Istanbul, taking just under three days for the journey.

THE SEASIDE

Scotland and Europe were playgrounds for the wealthy; ordinary people could not afford to go so far from home, but almost anyone could get to the seaside, which became a major goal for pleasure seekers. Naturally the scientists found a good reason for this. At the seaside you could breathe the health-giving ozone.

The gas ozone, actually a poisonous form of oxygen, had been discovered in 1839 and had been shown to be a good disinfectant. Because it also had a characteristic smell often associated with electrical discharges, it was thought to be healthy. The smell of slightly decomposing seaweed is rather similar, and so people jumped to the conclusion that sea air was especially beneficial – and this idea persists to this day.

In 1865 Dr T. Herbert Baker wrote to *The Times*: 'There can be little doubt that ozone is Nature's grand atmospheric disinfectant. All the facts which have hitherto been developed tend to prove this,' and he pointed out that no ozone is found near cesspools, nor downwind of cowsheds, nor in crowded churches. After reading this letter, W.S. Gilbert, who later became famous for his lyrics in the Gilbert and Sullivan operettas, wrote a poem about ozone, which begins as follows ('ohone' is a Scottish and Irish word for 'alas'):

Did you hear of the use of ozone, ohone?
It's the best disinfectant that's known, they've shown.
Though it doesn't appear
To my mind very clear,
Yet we'll sing of the praise of ozone, ohone!
Oh! We'll sing of the praise of ozone!

I don't see quite how it can act – in fact
In a room where a hundred are packed it's lacked:
In a tenanted place
Not a ghost of a trace
Of the gas that is known as ozone is shown,
Not a trace of this useful ozone!

The seriously adventurous traveller to the seaside might follow the practice of the royal family and brave the exhilarating new experience of sea bathing, which some doctors asserted was extraordinarily healthy, especially if the water was shockingly cold. Many used bathing machines, to avoid exposing themselves to the elements for more that the shortest possible time

ABOVE
Bathing machines
in use at Margate.

and to have expert help in case of some unimaginable disaster. In the smarter resorts you could take to a bathing machine at the top of the beach, be wheeled down to the water's edge, and then have one or two strong and capable assistants help you to take an invigorating plunge. The most daring even tried the risqué business of nude sea bathing, allegedly introduced in Scarborough, where the sea always feels ice-cold. I tried it once.

Most people, however, were more cautious and would take the health-giving sea air by promenading either beside the beach or, even better, over the sea itself on one of the new piers that were sprouting from the coastline all around the country. Early piers were massive constructions, usually with a sort of island offshore connected to the beach by a narrow bridge. However, Eugenius Birch came up with a clever system based on screw piles. To support the pier he made wrought-iron pillars with a screw thread on the end, and then screwed each one directly through the sand or shingle into the bedrock. He could use as many pillars as he wanted, and so built novel piers all round the country. One of his best known and best loved was the West Pier at Brighton, now sadly in disrepair and home each night to several million starlings, but still an impressive construction. Another, still going strong, is the North Pier at Blackpool, crammed with amusements along its quarter-mile length, its cast-iron feet thickly coated with mussels. In all, Birch built fourteen piers, of which seven survive.

ABOVE RIGHT
The West Pier at Brighton (*c.*1880), built by Eugenius Birch.

Piers proliferated throughout the Victorian period; by 1900 there were eighty of them, offering not only bands and promenades but also Punch-and-Judy stands, singers, dancers and jugglers in end-of-the-pier shows, steamer excursions, and all manner of other entertainments.

In 1800 Blackpool was a sleepy little seaside town with 700 inhabitants and four pubs, alongside a peaty stream that flows into the sea. Supplies came in twice a week on a cart from Preston, 18 miles away. However, the Victorians changed all that. People with jobs in factories had some spare time and spare cash, they wanted to enjoy themselves, and the new railways took them to the seaside. Blackpool changed within a generation to become the leisure capital of the north, a rambling monstrosity of hotels, boarding houses, entertainment centres, fast-food stalls and amusement arcades, all strung out along a mile or two of sandy beach – and it hardly seems to have changed since!

Hiram Maxim, who made a fortune by producing the world's first practical machine gun in 1884, also played a part in Blackpool's development as a leisure attraction. Apart from machine guns, he was interested in flying, and built a monster steam-powered biplane. Three men stood on a wooden platform, shovelling coal into the bowels of the huge steam engine. The ten-foot propellers howled into action, blowing away most of a nearby hayrick, and the machine thundered along its launch rails, briefly leaving them by perhaps three inches before plunging back down in a whirlwind of self-destruction. Maxim then gave up trying to fly for real, and built a wonderful fairground ride at Blackpool, in which a huge steam engine swung ten 'boats' on chains around a central pole, until they all flew out at a crazy angle, giving their occupants a dizzying view of the world. And although the steam engine is no more, you can still go on the ride today.

Almost everything about the seaside is Victorian, from buckets and spades to ice cream and piers. Even the deck chair was first mentioned in a P&O brochure of the time as the best place to relax on deck while travelling at sea. There were, however, occasional class problems at the seaside. It attracted both the genteel and the rough, and there were sometimes cases of drunken and boorish behaviour, but the emerging middle classes were determined to make the seaside a symbol of pleasure. It was glorified in countless paintings and photographs, partly because it was attractive and different, but mainly because it represented shared pleasure – an emblem of the perfect family, which was one of the icons of Victorian life.

'Halfpenny ices'. Street vendors were quick to exploit this new refreshment.

ICE CREAM

Towards the end of the century ice cream became a popular Victorian treat, thanks largely to a splendid and famous cook, Agnes Marshall, the Delia Smith of the 1880s and 1890s. She opened a cookery school in London in 1883 and sold her own equipment, especially freezers, which she claimed to have invented herself. She also seems to have made the first ice cream cone or cornet, around 1888.

She gave spectacular lecture demonstrations of her cookery, contributed weekly articles to a magazine called *The Table* and wrote four

books, of which the second and third were general cookery books, but the first and last were all about ice cream. Here is the recipe for her 'very rich' ice cream from the first of those books, *The Book of Ices*:

---

1 PINT OF CREAM

A QUARTER OF A POUND OF CASTOR SUGAR

8 YOLKS OF EGGS

Put the cream in a pan over the fire, and let it come to the boil,
and then pour it on to the sugar and yolks in a basin and mix well.
Return it to the pan and keep it stirred over the fire till it thickens and
clings well to the spoon, but do not let it boil: then pass it through a tammy,
or hair sieve, or strainer. Let it cool. Add vanilla or other flavour,
and freeze. Mould if desired. When partly frozen, half a pint
of whipped cream slightly sweetened may be added …

To freeze the mixture she took a wooden tub and packed the bottom with a mixture of crushed ice and salt, which takes the temperature down to about -18°C/0°F. Then she put on the ice her patent freezer, which was an aluminium drum that fitted into the tub with a gap all round of about half an inch to be filled with the ice and salt. Into the freezer went the mixture above, and by turning the handle on top she continually mixed the contents and scraped the slowly freezing mixture off the cold walls, so that perfect soft ice cream collected on the rotating paddle in the centre. After perhaps ten minutes the ice cream was ready to eat – and delicious, if the one I tried is anything to go by.

Mrs Agnes Marshall's
patent ice-cream freezer.

Steam-powered
roundabout,
in the style of Fred
Savage's gallopers.

FUNFAIRS

The industrial revolution changed Britain in many ways. Not only did people migrate from fields to factories and from the country into the town, they also acquired spending money and leisure time, which spurred on the entertainment business. Those who lived in the country could not easily get into town to be entertained, so the entertainment often travelled out to the country. In the south of England the first fair of the year was traditionally held in King's Lynn on 14 February, St Valentine's Day – and it still is. The Tuesday Market Place is crammed with helter-skelter, wall of death, roundabouts, haunted houses, terrifying rides, coconut shies, hoop-la, and peaceful stalls selling hot dogs and candy floss.

In 2001 the Lynn Mart was officially opened by the Mayor of King's Lynn from the steps of the dodgem cars in the presence of sixteen other mayors, accompanied by their deputy mayors, mace-bearers, sword-bearers and spouses, not to mention the Assistant Chief Constable, the head of the local fire brigade and other dignitaries. When the speeches were over, they all piled into the dodgems and charged after one another, mayoral robes and chains flying. The Assistant Chief Constable admitted afterwards that he had driven without due care and attention, exceeded the speed limit and gone the wrong way down a one-way street!

Fairs have been around for hundreds of years, but like so many aspects of life they were changed by the industrial revolution, and one of the principal instigators of this particular change was a self-made Norfolk man, Frederick Savage. His father had been deported to Tasmania for poaching when Fred was ten; he never went to school but earned his living as a lad by casual farm work, including one period of rook-scaring, at half a crown a week. However, he found one job he really enjoyed with a company that repaired agricultural machinery, and that was to be his future.

In 1851 Savage moved to King's Lynn and set up his own business in St Nicholas Street, on the corner of the Tuesday Market Place. He began modestly, making hoes and rakes, but soon realised that the future of agriculture lay in machines, especially if they could be steam-powered. He invented some of his own, including a steam plough that rivalled Fowler's (see p. 26), a harvesting machine and a colossal self-propelled steam engine, the Juggernaut, that could drive out to a field, do all the threshing and then drive back with the sacks of grain.

Because his workshop was on the corner of the Tuesday Market Place, the showmen who came to the Lynn Mart often brought their machines to him for repair after the winter, and he became as knowledgeable as the owners about the fairground rides. An inventive chap, he soon came up with improvements to the existing rides, and even with new ones of his own design. One of his early rides was the Velocipede, which was essentially half a dozen bicycles welded together in a circle. The bicycle had become immensely popular from about 1860, and the Velocipede was a hit too; the only problem arose when the local cycling club turned up, paid for a ride and then pedalled enthusiastically round and round for an hour, preventing anyone else from having a go!

Savage progressed from the Velocipede to more complex and spectacular rides, of which probably the most famous was the Gallopers, a roundabout with magnificent horses that rose and fell majestically on twisted brass poles. This was a ride that anyone could enjoy – one for the whole family. The horses were sometimes replaced by cockerels, geese, even turkeys, but the principle remained the same – a gentle round-and-round and up-and-down movement, which was so popular that even today there are a few sets of Gallopers in operation, and many modern fairground rides are based on similar simple movements.

His other great success was the Gondolas (pronounced with the accent on the second syllable). These were a string of half a dozen 'boats', elegantly festooned with brass and gilt carvings, which chased one another round and round on rails on a steep switchback course, each carrying up to four couples in cosy pairs of red velvet seats. Early versions of this ride proved dangerous: the humps were so sharp that at full speed the gondolas tended to come off the rails at the top. Savage's solution to this problem was to lay a third rail to take one of the outside wheels of each gondola, in order to keep it on a slightly more even keel. This third rail became known as 'Savage's bottom'.

Savage's genius lay not so much in inventing brand-new rides as in spotting the best features of existing ones and greatly improving them. Before he came along, roundabouts had been pushed round by a man or a donkey, so they tended to get slower and slower as the day wore on. Savage pioneered a major step forward by using steam engines to drive many of the rides. Next he introduced the idea of the centre engine; the steam engine that drove the folded-up ride along the road remained in place and the ride unfolded around it like the petals of a flower. The engine sat in the middle, out of harm's way, and provided power both for the ride and for the organ that supplied the music.

Savage took great pride in every stage of the work. He never learned to read or write but had such a clear idea of what he wanted that, by making a few scratches with a stick in the dust on the workshop floor, he could pass on instructions to his workers. He employed carpenters, skilled woodcarvers, blacksmiths, painters and many others. Indeed, he was proud of the fact that at St Nicholas Street they made every single part of the wonderful horses for his Gallopers except for the horsehair tails and the glass eyes. He was a benevolent employer and a popular citizen, and not only did the people elect him Mayor of King's Lynn, but within his lifetime they erected a fine statue of him in his mayoral robes, welcoming visitors in through the south gate of the town.

THEATRES AND MUSIC HALLS

Funfairs visited towns, where the pickings might be richer, but townies were less dependent on them than the country folk, since the towns had their own fixed places of entertainment in the theatres and music halls. The theatre had become much more respectable since David Garrick cleaned up the Theatre Royal, Drury Lane, in the late 1700s; he had, for example, stopped the previously common practice of men going backstage to watch the actresses undressing and putting on their costumes.

1890s advertisement
for Buffalo Bill's
Wild West Show.

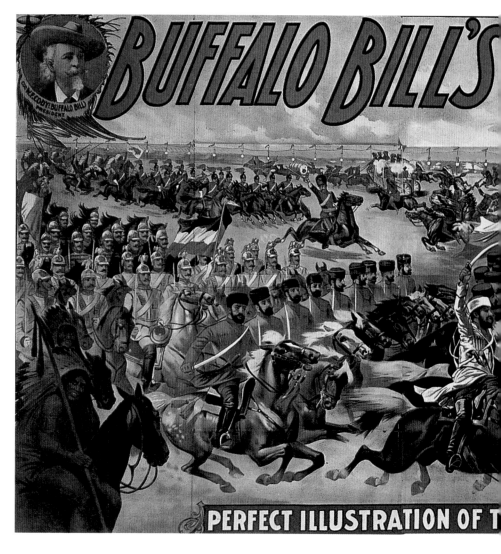

New plays were written for the masses – well, at least for the middle class
– and the melodrama became a great success. Smart theatres were fre-
quented by the well to do; the cheapest seats might cost a shilling. People
with only a few pennies to spend might go instead to a music hall.

Many music halls started life as pubs, where the regulars enjoyed singing
and putting on other sorts of entertainment. If the landlord saw the opportunity for progress and could raise the capital, he could build a large room
on to the side of the pub, and hire acts to attract more customers. These
included singers, dancers, jugglers, acrobats, comics and actors performing
short sketches. Some music halls developed into regular theatres, though
without offering serious plays. Others remained more like the northern vari-

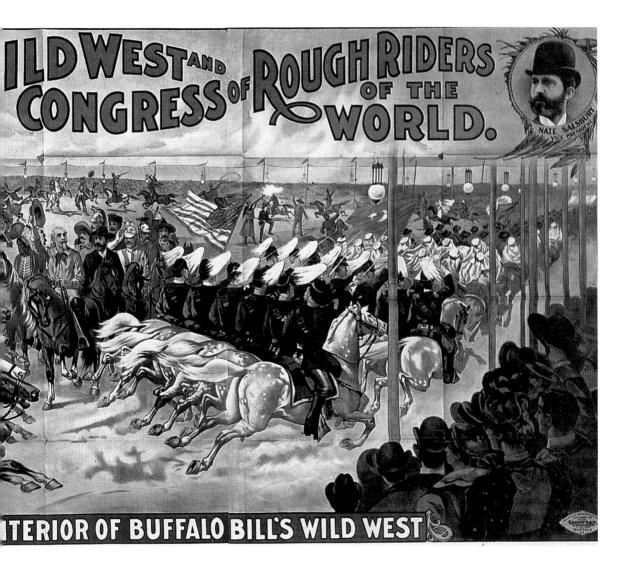

ety clubs of the twentieth century — large pubs with a stage and many tables where the customers could eat and drink while watching the performance.

Occasionally a really grand show would hit town, and among the most famous was Buffalo Bill's Wild West Show. William Frederick Cody, born in Iowa in 1846, became a rider in the brand new Pony Express when he was fourteen and an army scout during the American Civil War. In 1865 he contracted to supply the workers on the Kansas Pacific Railroad with bison meat, and in eighteen months claimed he had killed 4,000 bison, commonly called buffalo, which was how he came to be nicknamed Buffalo Bill. In 1883 he organised the Wild West Show, starring himself, Big Chief Sitting Bull and sharpshooter Annie Oakley. This representation of life on the plains toured Europe and the United States for twenty years. The Queen was a great fan; she asked for a special performance at Windsor, and several members of the family joined in!

STAGE LIGHTING

One reason for the growing popularity of theatrical performances was the steadily improving quality of the technical support, and in particular the lighting. Gas lighting had been around since 1800 but provided a poor flickering glimmer that hardly lit up the actors. In 1809 Humphry Davy invented the arc lamp, which was basically just two carbon rods, each connected to one side of a battery and then brought together to make a short circuit. When the rods are taken to perhaps a millimetre apart, an intense electrical spark – an arc – flows between them and generates an immensely bright light, the same sort of brilliant white light as you get from a welding torch.

The arc lamp was by far the brightest artificial light anyone had ever seen, and arc lamps were used in lighthouses, in projectors for magic lanterns, at the Paris Opéra, and later for film projectors and for street lighting. They had problems: in particular the arc evaporated tiny pieces of carbon from the rods, so that they were gradually used up and had to be continually manipulated to stay a short distance apart. This could be done with a clockwork motor, but the mechanism was tricky. Also the arc took a high current and quickly exhausted the rather primitive batteries that existed in the first half of the nineteenth century. However, they became more popular towards the end of the century, with the advent of electrical generators that could supply the power needed, and it is said that by 1884 the United States was lit up at night with 90,000 arc lamps.

In the theatre limelight provided more useful illumination. First discovered by the Cornishman Goldsworthy Gurney in 1826, limelight was sometimes called the Drummond Light, because during a survey of Ireland Thomas Drummond found that when he used limelight with a parabolic reflector he could signal 95 miles from Antrim to Ben Lomond. In the early 1820s Gurney had invented an oxygen-hydrogen blowpipe, which produced an exceedingly hot flame, and he began experimenting with various materials to see what he could do with it. He discovered that when he played this flame on to lime, especially with a little added magnesia, it produced an intense white light. Today the simplest material to use is a stick of blackboard chalk; when introduced into the oxygen-hydrogen flame, it quickly begins to glow, and within a few seconds the light becomes dazzling – not as fierce or blinding as an arc light, but nevertheless extremely bright. As with the arc lamp, there are some problems, because the lime is gradually burned away, but limelight is much easier to handle than an arc lamp and it needs no electricity. By the 1860s limelight had become the standard for stage lighting, especially for the sun and for follow-spots – hence the phrase 'in the limelight'. Limelight was used in London theatres for fifty years, and to this day spotlights in theatres are known as 'limes'.

Making limelight using an oxy-hydrogen blowpipe and a piece of limestone.

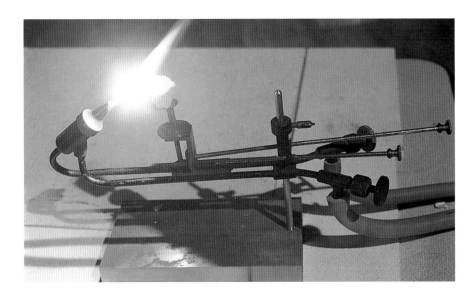

Alongside this developing technology there arose a new type of entertainment, based on the growing general interest in science, and in some cases theatre acts were built around scientific tricks. A splendid example of this was Pepper's Ghost, which was invented by Henry Dircks around 1858 and first demonstrated on Christmas Eve 1862 at the Royal Polytechnic in London's Regent Street by 'Professor' John Henry Pepper, a lecturer in chemistry and an enthusiastic populariser of science.

Picture the scene. A dashing young man comes on to the stage and is suddenly confronted by a fearful spectre – a shimmering white ghost that appears in front of him from nowhere, floats above the floor and howls in a terrifying way. The hero, startled but brave, draws his sword and charges towards the ghost, which floats out of his way. There ensues a dramatic struggle until the hero manages to run his adversary through and through with his sword, and with a final blood-curdling shriek the ghost fades and disappears.

Pepper's theatrical
ghost, lit by limelight.

Here's how it worked. Below the stage a person draped in white sheets pranced about pretending to be a ghost. This ghost was out of sight of the audience but, when brilliantly lit by limelight, became visible as a reflection in a huge sheet of glass hung at an angle across the front of the stage, and it appeared to the audience to be on the stage or even floating just above it. So when the limelight was suddenly switched on, the ghost would magically appear from nowhere. During the struggle the hero was on the stage and the ghost beneath it, so they never got anywhere near one another. At the climax, when the hero 'killed' the ghost, the limelight was switched off or slowly covered over, so that the ghost slowly disappeared.

This act must have been tricky to do, since neither of the performers could see the illusion; so they must have spent a great deal of time rehearsing, with the director shouting instructions from a seat in the audience. There were technical drawbacks, too: getting the huge sheet of glass in place was a complicated operation, and the hero was inaudible behind it, so in effect the audience could hear only the ghost. However, for an audience who had not seen it before, the effect must have been astonishing; *The Times* described it as the most wonderful illusion ever put before the public. It certainly impressed the Prince and Princess of Wales, and the ghost was summoned to Windsor Castle. This was one of the first uses of science to create a special effect of the type that so dominates the cinema today.

On the other hand, people were fascinated by science itself and wanted to know what it was all about. The wonders of electricity and new chemistry being investigated and paraded by the famous scientists of the day brought crowds flocking to hear them lecture. Humphry Davy, the dashing Cornishman with flashing eyes and dark curly hair, and Michael Faraday, the Yorkshire blacksmith's son who never went to school but became one of the greatest scientists of his day, became seriously famous. Davy delivered such popular talks at the Royal Institution that there were tremendous traffic jams in Albemarle Street, and as a result it became the first one-way street in London.

RUBBER

Raw rubber, or 'caoutchouc' as it was called, was elastic, sticky and interesting, but difficult to handle and not of much use. Joseph Priestley had pointed out in 1770 that it was good for rubbing out pencil marks, which was how it came also to be called 'rubber', and in the early 1800s various people had found ways to combine rubber with other materials to make soles for shoes, elastic garters and waterproof clothing, including the mackintosh, pioneered by Glaswegian Charles McIntosh and first manufactured in Manchester in 1824.

Charles Goodyear, a hardware merchant in Philadelphia, saw the importance of rubber, and tried all sorts of processes to convert the sticky raw material into a useful product. Around 1840 he accidentally overheated a mixture of rubber, sulphur and white lead, and found that although some of the material had burned, part of it had become just what he was looking for. Further experiments showed that the sulphur was the critical additive; heating raw rubber with sulphur turned it into a much stronger and more manageable material. The process was called 'vulcanisation' from Vulcan, the Roman god of fire.

Surprisingly, the Americans failed to capitalise on this discovery, and even though the French had done much of the early pioneering work, including bringing raw rubber back from the tropics, the British now took over and began to manufacture rubber on a large scale. World rubber production took off; exports of the raw material from Brazil increased from 31 tons in 1827 to 28,000 tons in 1900, by which time Britain was importing 20,000 tons a year.

Originally all this rubber came from South America, but it became clear that demand would soon outstrip the South American supply, and the India Office sent half a dozen rubber tree seedlings to Calcutta in 1873. They died, and only after an English planter on the Amazon had sent seeds to Kew Gardens, where they were sown and carefully nurtured, was it possible to send 2,000 plants to Ceylon in August 1877. From there they were sent on to Singapore, and by about 1895 the rubber plantations of the Far East came into serious production – a fine example of Victorian progress through the Empire.

John Boyd Dunlop, riding on his pneumatic tyres.

The vulcanisation of rubber led to all sorts of new possibilities. A substantial chunk of the expanding rubber business was in transport. Solid rubber tyres were used for carriages and other vehicles, and in 1845 Robert Thomson from Stonehaven patented what he called 'aerial wheels': 'an elastic bearing for the purpose of lessening the power required to draw carriages, rendering their motion easier and diminishing the noise they make when in motion', in other words pneumatic tyres. He made his tyres from tubes of canvas impregnated with rubber and coated with leather, and intended them for use on horse-drawn and steam carriages. Because people were sceptical about them, he arranged for a scientific trial in Regent's Park in London.

He took two identical carriages, one with conventional wooden wheels and iron tyres, the other fitted with his aerial wheels, and measured the force or 'draught' needed to pull them on a good smooth road. The first thing everyone noticed was that his aerial tyres ran quietly, while the iron tyres made a loud grinding, scrunching noise as they rolled along. His silent carriage caused quite a stir among the crowds in the park, and prompted lengthy discussions in the *Mechanics Magazine*, which concluded:

> Despite the opinion most people would form … that the draught must be
> greatly increased, [it] is unquestionably much lessened. The tyres are
> perfectly elastic as well as soft. They do not retard the carriage – they yield
> to every obstacle, permit the carriage to pass over it without rising up, and
> expanding as they pass from the obstruction, return the force borrowed for a
> moment to compress the tyre.

However, even though Thomson's tyres were clearly a great step forward, the world was not yet ready for them, partly because in the 1840s rubber was a fairly expensive material, and they disappeared without trace. Forty years later, a Scottish vet living in Belfast reinvented pneumatic tyres and made himself a fortune.

John Boyd Dunlop's young son Johnny liked to ride a tricycle to school

but complained that the cobbled streets made his bottom sore, so John Boyd fitted his wheels with tyres made of rubber tubes inflated with air and nailed to the wooden rims, so the story goes, with strips of cloth torn from one of his wife's old dresses. The effect was instant; not only did Johnny stop complaining about his sore bottom, he also beat all his friends when they raced. Clearly these pneumatic tyres might have a future, and John Boyd managed to convince the world by persuading Willie Hume to give them a try.

Willie Hume, Captain of the Belfast Cruisers Cycle Club, had taken to riding a 'safety bicycle' after a terrible crash on his high bicycle or penny-farthing, and was intrigued to hear about these new tyres. He tried them out on the quiet, and then took them along on 18 May 1889 to a race at the Queen's College playing fields. Everyone laughed at him when they saw he was using not only a namby-pamby safety bike but also the squishy new tyres, but they stopped laughing when he won the race. Two of the losers in that race were the Du Cros brothers, whose dad Harvey was a wealthy paper merchant. When they saw what could be done on pneumatic tyres they wanted them too. The same summer they took pneumatic tyres to England, won every race they were allowed to enter, and put Dunlop tyres on the map. In 1896 Harvey Du Cros bought the rights for £3 million.

Rubber had found more entertaining uses, too. In 1824 Michael Faraday discovered that by laying one sheet of raw rubber on top of another and pressing the edges together he could make gas-tight containers, ideal for containing the hydrogen gas with which he was experimenting. 'The caoutchouc is exceedingly elastic,' he wrote in the *Quarterly Journal of Science*. 'Bags made of it have been expanded by having air forced into them, until the caoutchouc was quite transparent, and when expanded by hydrogen they were so light as to form balloons with considerable lifting power.' Toy rubber balloons were introduced the following year in the form of a messy-sounding kit, and vulcanised rubber balloons – almost like those you can buy today – were first made by J.G. Ingram of London in 1847.

LAWNS AND PARKS

During the early 1800s a large country house like Blenheim Palace would have employed up to fifty 'mowers' – men with scythes who would go out on summer days at four in the morning and walk in line abreast to cut the grass short. Scything works best when the grass is heavy with dew, which was why they started so early in the morning. Then in 1830 Edwin Beard Budding patented a lawn-mower, a machine that one person could push and cut the grass – and everything changed. As Budding wrote in his patent application, 'Country gentlemen may find in using my machine themselves an amusing, useful and healthy exercise,' and he was right; his idea caught on.

Ransomes of Ipswich were soon selling the Budding mowing machine, and proclaimed in their advertising: 'This machine is so easy to manage, that persons unpractised in the Art of Mowing, may cut the Grass on Lawns, Pleasure Grounds, and Bowling Greens with ease.' And they produced a splendidly clear set of instructions: 'take hold of the handles, as in driving a barrow … push the machine steadily forward along the greensward, without lifting the handles, but rather exerting a moderate pressure downwards.'

The mowing machine may have seemed just like many other Victorian gadgets, but it had several long-lasting effects. First, the new affluent middle class could now have lawns – patches of smooth grass in their gardens where the ladies could take tea in the summer. Second, they could use some of their leisure time in playing games. Lawn tennis (see p. 162) had appeared as a derivative of real or royal tennis, now that rubber had been vulcanised and rubber balls were available. Cricket acquired smooth new pitches; golf acquired velvety new greens. Bowling, croquet and many other games and sports became possible, or at least more predictable and therefore much better fun. Tennis and croquet especially became important in the elaborate Victorian courtship rituals, for young men and women could, with perfect decorum, share afternoons on the green grass and so try out the concept of shared pleasure, the prerequisite for happy family life.

Budding's mowing machine. As he put it, 'Country gentlemen may find in using my machine themselves an amusing, useful and healthy exercise.'

A Select Committee on Public Walks had suggested in 1833 that providing parks for the poor of London would encourage them to give up drinking houses, dog fights, boxing matches and other debasing pleasures, and instead take up walking, ball games and other healthy pursuits. To some extent this moral crusade worked; for example, thousands of tons of mud and gravel were brought upriver by barge from the newly dredged docks to raise the level of the marsh at

Battersea, and when Battersea Park was opened in 1858 it was quickly filled by people playing cricket, football and rounders.

Both the lawn and the park helped in the development of a new form of middle-class family entertainment – the picnic. Posh people were used to picnics; at Eton's annual celebration of the Fourth of June picnic hampers must for generations have been produced from their carriages for the great and the good and their children to sip champagne and eat sumptuous food. The middle-class picnic would more likely have been based round sandwiches and beer, or lemonade for the children, but the idea of eating in the open air had spread, like the butter on the bread and the blanket on the new-mown grass.

THE WITHDRAWING ROOM

After dinner the family would withdraw from the dining room to the withdrawing room, or drawing room, for the evening's entertainment, which would often mean music. The flickering gaslight that lit most middle-class homes made reading rather difficult, and many families settled for evenings round the piano. Pianos became almost mandatory for every aspirational drawing room, and in the large families – ten children were not unusual – there would always be someone to play and someone to sing.

Popular music flourished. Their appetites whetted at the music hall or the fairground, people rushed out to buy the sheet music for the latest hit tunes, in order to practise them at home. And if no one in the house was able to play the piano there was the pianola. At first these were separate pieces of equipment that you could push up to your piano. The wooden fingers lay over the piano keys, and as the punched paper roll that carried the instructions was pulled round by the mechanism, so the wooden fingers were pulled down and played the piano keys like human fingers. This meant that anyone could have real piano music in their homes, and entertain their friends and neighbours. Later the pianola was incorporated into the piano itself, so you had to buy only a single machine, which you could either play yourself or set on 'auto'. Naturally all the popular tunes became available on the paper rolls for pianolas, and anyone could hear them.

Also immensely popular was the musical box. Some small toy musical boxes displayed their brass drums with the fixed pins that twanged the resonant tongues of brass, revealing their mechanism for the world to see. Others were artfully concealed in jewellery boxes, and played a pretty

In the withdrawing room, after dinner.

tune when the lid was opened. However, there were also great lumbering Jeroboam musical boxes that would rival the piano in the drawing room. They had trumpets and cymbals, curtseying fairies and whirling dervishes, and like a modern CD player they would play any of ten tunes in any order you wanted. No middle-class house need be without music: yet another example of the progress brought by technology.

During the early 1800s young ladies were expected to be accomplished not only at music but also as artists; drawing and painting were important social skills. By the middle of the century the advent of photography was making pictures much more readily available, and the smart way to display them was with a magic lantern show. Limelight was used to project pictures from glass slides on to a screen or wall, and this allowed the Victorian equivalent of the family slide show. Magic lanterns for projecting pictures had been around for a long time, but the availability of really bright light and photographic images, printed as positives on glass plates, made the magic lantern far more popular. In Philadelphia the brothers William and Frederick Langenheim took out a patent on these positive glass plates in 1850, and won a medal at the Great Exhibition in 1851.

PHOTOGRAPHY

Tom Wedgwood, son of potter Josiah Wedgwood, took the first photographs in 1802 at Etruria, the family factory. Tom was a sickly lad, and died at the age of thirty-four, but he must have been a charming man; Sydney Smith said that he knew 'no man who appears to have made such an impression on his friends'. Wedgwood painted leather or paper with a solution of silver nitrate, which is sensitive to light. He placed leaves or ferns on top, and exposed the specimen to sunlight for perhaps half an hour. The light turns the exposed silver nitrate to silver metal, which looks black under those conditions, so the shape of the leaf was marked by a light silhouette.

An original by Anna Atkins, the first person to use photographs in a book, which was published in 1841.

Wedgwood never found a way of 'fixing' his photographs; when exposed to light the whole thing gradually darkened until the silhouette was no longer visible. Nevertheless some were kept in the dark at the Royal Society for about a hundred years – interested researchers occasionally peered at them for a few seconds by candlelight – before they lost their images completely.

The next strides forward seem to have been taken by Frenchmen: Joseph Nicéphore de Niepce produced pictures on bitumen in 1827, and Louis Jaques Mandé Daguerre produced beautiful crisp pictures on silver plates, which came to be called daguerreotypes, and were shown to the French Academy of Sciences on 7 January 1839. The daguerreotypes were rich with fine, clear detail, but alas each was small and only a single piece; there was no way of making copies.

Meanwhile John Herschel and William Henry Fox Talbot had been experimenting in England and eventually came up with the processes that were to dominate photography for 150 years. First John Herschel invented the cyanotype process, which was simpler and cheaper than the silver-based system, and easy to use. The only problem was that the pictures came out bright blue, which made them unsuitable for some subjects, including portraits. A friend of Herschel's, Anna Atkins, used cyanotypes in her book about seaweed, published in 1841; it was the first book in the world to be illustrated with photographs.

Henry Talbot pursued the silver-based process and, generally following Herschel's lead, steadily improved the fixing and developing of the negatives, and the printing of positives from them. One of the great advantages of this system over the daguerreotype was that from a negative Talbot could make any number of positive prints. In 1844 he published a fine book, *The Pencil of Nature*, in which he explained his methods and illustrated them with his photographs. Unfortunately he also patented the whole process, even though he had not really invented any part of it, and his patent held up the progress of photography for some ten years, until in 1853 he was persuaded by the Presidents of the Royal Society and the Royal Academy to let his patent lapse.

As the processes became simpler and cheaper, the photograph grew ever more popular, particularly in the shape of the carte-de-visite. This was like a normal visiting card but with a portrait of the person on the back. Because they were cheap, most people could have portraits of family and loved ones on the mantelpiece, but the rich loved it too. In July 1860 the Queen had portraits taken of herself, Albert and the children, which were then published as the *Royal Album*, and sold in millions. For the first time ever, people really knew what the royal family looked like. And when Albert died in the following year, 70,000 of his cartes-de-visite sold in a single week. The photographers

A royal family *carte de visite*.

One of Henry Talbot's original cameras.

soon cashed in on this new enthusiasm, and collecting cartes-de-visite became a national hobby. The age of celebrities had arrived.

The picture postcard was born in Germany in 1872, but unfortunately British Post Office regulations prohibited the use of any but plain cards until 1894, and so in the UK picture postcards did not really become popular until the early 1900s.

Taking photographs remained a rather messy and complicated business, although hundreds of enthusiasts did it and thousands of pictures were taken, until George Eastman produced a paper-roll-film camera in 1887, soon followed by his Kodak. With this point-and-shoot box camera, anyone could take a hundred pictures and then send the whole camera back to the factory for processing. 'You press the button; we do the rest.'

Colour photography was invented by the eminent Scottish scientist James Clerk Maxwell, who became the first Professor of Experimental Physics at Cambridge and died in 1879, the year that Albert Einstein was born. Maxwell worked out by a series of ingenious experiments that the basic colours are red, blue and green: by mixing these in suitable proportions you can make any other colours. He then applied this idea in a typically brilliant way.

Colour film did not exist, but he was able to make a colour photograph of a piece of ribbon by taking three black-and-white photographs, one through a red filter, one through a blue filter, and one through a green filter. He made a positive glass plate of each photograph and then projected them all at the same time, on to the same screen and through the same-coloured filters. The red part of the ribbon had appeared bright on the picture taken through a red filter, and therefore showed red on projection, because more red light hit the screen than any other, and the same principle applied to all the colours of the ribbon. As a result the final projected image was in astonishing colour. An American called Ives tried to sell this system in the 1890s, but colour photography did not really take off until the Lumière Brothers patented a simple one-shot colour plate.

MOVING PICTURES

The idea of pictures that move must always have been appealing, and a number of Victorian toys were produced to create the effect of movement. These ranged from the simple 'flip book' to spinning drums with pictures opposite slits in the side or arranged opposite mirrors, in such a way that the viewer peering in would see a rapid succession of images that would convey the impression of continuous movement. These toys had a variety of names that sounded scientific – zoeoscope, praxinoscope (see p. 44) and so on, but they all relied on the same basic principle.

There is much controversy about the first continuous moving pictures, or 'film' as we call it today. The pictures don't really move; each film or television programme is made of a series of still pictures, shown in rapid succession, which gives the impression of moving pictures. The difficulty was first to take a large number of pictures quickly in rapid succession and then to project the resulting positives, also in rapid succession.

Eadweard Muybridge (see p. 41) showed what appeared to be moving pictures in 1885, but they were taken with a large number of separate cameras, lined up side by side, so the successive pictures each had a slightly different viewpoint. Also his complicated projection system allowed only for a dozen or so pictures to be shown, and in any case the pictures had to be painted by an artist on to the disc for the projector; they were not the original prints.

In my opinion the first real moving pictures were taken by Louis Aimé Augustin le Prince, a Frenchman working in Leeds during the 1880s. In October 1888 he used a single camera to take a succession of photographs of Leeds Bridge, from the window of a building at one end of the bridge. He printed these as positives on glass plates, several of which still exist; they show people walking and a horse pulling a cart towards the camera. He had a plan for a projector, in which the glass slides would slide down a spiral chute to pause one after another in rapid succession in front of the lens, and so give the appearance of continuous motion.

Le Prince wanted to sell his invention in America; Edison was known to be interested. He had some of his possessions boxed ready for shipment, but before leaving he went over to France to tidy up some family business. On 16 September 1890 at Dijon station he was seen off by his brother Albert on a train bound for Paris, but he was never seen again. Police made extensive enquiries, but no trace was ever found of le Prince, his luggage or the equipment he had with him.

William Friese-Greene also took moving pictures in Bristol, but he never succeeded in taking or showing them in rapid enough succession, and it was left to several other people, notably the Lumière Brothers and Thomas Edison, to make the first effective motion pictures. The Regent Street Polytechnic, where Pepper's Ghost had first appeared, was also where the British public first paid to see Lumière motion pictures on 20 February 1896.

CHAPTER FIVE

HEALTH AND HAPPINESS

The velocipede shower, or *vélo-douche* (see p. 135) – ideal for getting fit and clean at the same time!

WHEN VICTORIA CAME to the throne, the nation's health was poor, by today's standards. In towns the infant mortality rate was 50 per cent; that is, only half of all the babies who were born lived to see their fifth birthdays. The prime reason for this appalling death rate was contamination of the water supplies. This gave rise to cholera, typhoid or simply diarrhoea, because the sewage was not properly separated from the drinking water. Many developing countries still suffer from this problem, but only with hindsight can we see how unhealthy the Victorians were.

To some extent Victorian Britain was a nation of double standards: the rich had better food and better conditions, while the poor were always struggling for existence, and this divide grew worse as the industrial revolution developed and the rich became richer still. Therefore it became socially necessary to show off what wealth you had, just to demonstrate how happy and healthy you were; and one thing Victorians were really good at was showing off. The houses had to be grand, and there had to be servants; and above all you had to have clever possessions, and gadgets.

VICTORIAN GADGETRY

The Victorians loved their gadgets; in 1837 only 259 applications were taken out for new inventions, but by the end of the century there were 25,000 patent applications every year. Bicycles became immensely popular from about the 1860s, and there were monocycles and dicycles and tricycles and high bicycles and safety bicycles and 'sociables' – bicycles made for three – not to mention hand-cranked velocipedes and bicycles made entirely from cane and string. There were brushes to clean the chain, driving propellers on the handlebars, and inflatable saddles to 'protect the organic parts'. There were water cycles and underwater cycles and even flying cycles, at least in the imagination of the inventors!

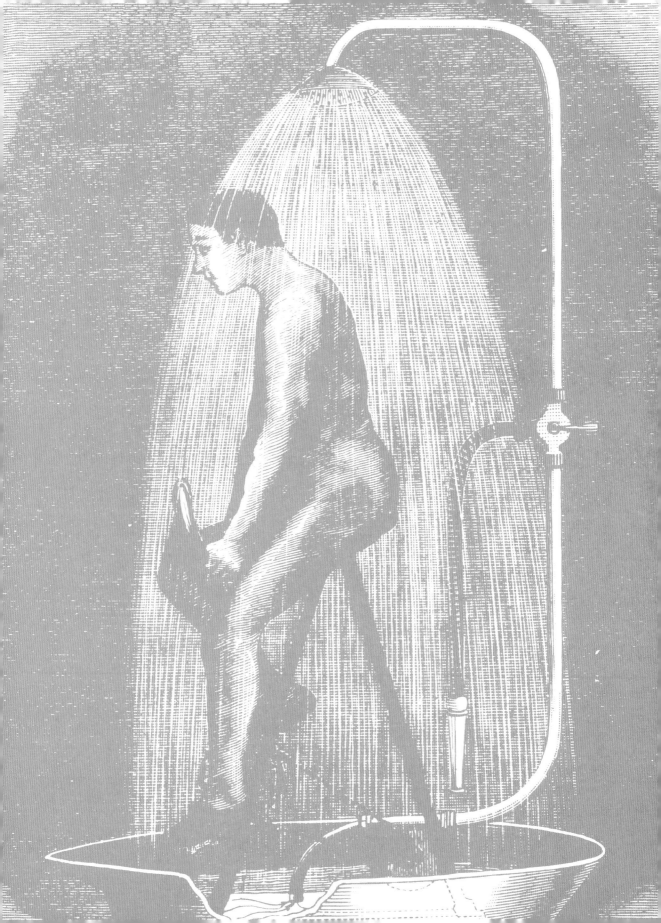

1886 advertisement
from the *Illustrated
London News*.

The bicycle even came into the house, in the shape of a velocipede shower made in England and demonstrated as the *vélo-douche* at the Paris Exhibition of 1897.

> This device combines the morning wash with a means of keeping in training, and remaining in condition, in a truly ideal way. It is, in fact, a combination of a bicycle and a shower-bath which does not waste the driving power created by pedalling, but uses it to drive a rotating pump which forces water up from a tank. The harder one pedals, the more powerful the flow of water ... The *vélo-douche* will prove a particular asset in the cycling clubs and cycling schools which have been set up in such numbers.

I tried a *vélo-douche* myself, and found it easy to use and great fun – just the thing to have in the garden on a hot summer's day. To accommodate one inside would have needed a large bathroom, but then the large bathroom was coming in. Before Victoria's time, and for the lower classes, the bath was a zinc tub in front of the fire with water heated in the 'copper' on the kitchen range, but for the new middle classes there was piped water and main drains, and so there could be a bathroom with space for a bath, a basin, a new-fangled water-closet and even a *vélo-douche*. In the soap and perfumery section of the Great Exhibition of 1851 there were no fewer than 727 exhibitors, and in 1853 William Gladstone reduced the tax on soap from 50 per cent to nothing, which was encouraging for anyone wishing to wash. After all, cleanliness was next to godliness.

Throughout Victoria's reign, shaving meant a cut-throat razor, but this fearsome weapon was difficult to use on your own chin, so most men who could not afford to go to the barber for a shave were either bearded or frequently adorned with bloody nicks where the blade had strayed. Early safety razors were not much use, and a better design by Sam Henson, one time partner of John Stringfellow (see p. 18) did not catch on. The breakthrough came right at the end of the century, in the hands of a bottle-cap salesman from Wisconsin with the improbable name of King Camp Gillette.

Gillette was a man with a mission to improve the lot of the human race. He and his brothers invented several minor improvements for beer barrels, and then in 1893 he wrote a book called *The Human Drift*, in which he described his utopian vision of the future. He wanted to bring all the sixty million people in North America together to live in one colossal city, Metropolis. Forty thousand tower blocks would be built around Niagara Falls, and be powered by hydroelectric power from the falls.

Everyone would eat together in vast halls, each holding 1,500 diners. Because of all the new labour-saving devices, people would work only between the ages of twenty-five and thirty, and everyone would live happily ever after. It was an ultimate socialist dream.

Gillette's boss William Painter was rather scornful of such grand ideas and said that, if he wanted to make something of himself, Gillette should invent something that people would buy and throw away. One spring morning in 1895 he was struggling to shave with a blunt razor, and had his big idea – the disposable razor blade. He spent seven years developing the blade and finally got it in on the market in 1902. Ever since then we have lived in a throw-away society, for now we have disposable pens, disposable shopping bags, disposable nappies – and the trend began with King Camp Gillette in 1895.

The bathroom, however, was not alone in being filled with gadgets. In the drawing room would be a piano or pianola, musical boxes, cigar-cutters, electric matches (cigarette lighters) and perhaps a cabinet of curiosities for gentlemen to discuss. The kitchen would naturally have all the latest cooking utensils, with Mrs Beeton's book for guidance (see p. 173), and such gadgets as sugar snippers, knife sharpeners, nutmeg grinders and food mixers. Also downstairs would be a washing machine and perhaps even a dish-washing machine. Refrigerators powered by steam were used industrially, but domestic fridges did not really come into use until domestic electricity was readily available towards the end of the century. Naturally the well-to-do would experiment with the new exotic foods: fruits such as pineapples from the far reaches of the Empire, and Fortnum and Mason could sell you, for five shillings, a ready-to-eat roasted duck with green peas.

THE BIRTH OF THE BRAND

As more and more people migrated from the country into the towns a new problem surfaced with food. On the farm everyone had grown their own; it may have been meagre, but at least they knew what they were getting and where it had come from. In town they could not grow food, so they had to buy it, and where there was commerce there was corruption. Many a food seller was on the make, and all too often what people wanted was rather different from what they actually got. Bakers sometimes added powdered chalk to their poor flour in order to make it look whiter and to save money. Dairies watered down the milk and then added

A Victorian Fridge

We challenged refrigeration expert John Missenden to build a domestic refrigerator capable of keeping food chilled and also, if possible, of making ice cubes, using only Victorian technology, and in particular no electricity. He came up with a handsome hand-powered machine built essentially from two commodes connected by a miniature village pump, based on the design patented in 1857 by Jacob Perkins.

The working fluid, ether, is pumped round within a sealed system of pipes by a hand-operated force pump. The compressed ether vapour is pushed into the big box where it condenses into

liquid. As it turns into liquid it gives up latent heat and warms the water in the container. The liquid ether trickles on into the small drum. There the pump pulls on it, lowering the pressure, which makes the ether evaporate and cool down, just as you feel cool when you step out of a warm shower and the water evaporates from your skin. Technically this happens because each molecule of ether needs extra energy to escape from the liquid into the vapour. This extra energy is the latent heat of evaporation, and it has to be taken from the surroundings, so the second container cools down and would hold the food to be refrigerated. This is essentially how modern fridges work, although they use safer fluids – ether is dangerously flammable.

We tested the machine under tough conditions – in a steamy glasshouse at Kew Gardens on a hot summer day. After perhaps half an hour of pumping, which was quite hard work, I measured the temperature in each container, and found that the second was about 14°C cooler than the first. So the fridge was working, just about, although I would probably have had to keep pumping continuously day and night to keep food fresh, and I doubt if I could ever have made an ice cube. The principle was sound, but the machine could hardly have been practical, even if it had been properly insulated.

The first steam-powered industrial fridges appeared in 1858, and in due course enabled the shipping of such exotic food as lamb from New Zealand – Queen Victoria ate some – but the domestic fridge did not really catch on until there was a reliable supply of electricity at about the turn of the century.

RICH CHRISTMAS PUDDING.

½-lb. McDougall's Self-Raising Flour.
½-lb. Beef Suet. ½-lb. Raisins (stoned).
¼-lb. Currants. ½-lb. Sultanas.
½-lb. Moist Sugar. ¼-lb. Mixed Peel.
2-oz. Blanched Almonds. 1 Apple (peeled & cored).
Juice and Rind of 1 Lemon.
½ Nutmeg (grated).
¼ teaspoonful Ground Ginger.
¼ teaspoonful Mixed Spice.
¼ teaspoonful Salt. 4 Eggs.
½ gill Brandy. 1 gill Milk.

Chop the Suet, Raisins, Sultanas, Peel, Almonds and Apple, or pass separately through a mincing machine, and mix all the dry ingredients. Beat up the Eggs, add the Milk, and stir them with the Brandy and Lemon Juice to the Fruit, etc. Put the mixture into a greased mould, cover with a pudding cloth, place at once in boiling water, and boil for eight hours.

NOTE.—This pudding improves with keeping, when required for use it should be re-boiled for two or three hours.

FAMILY CHRISTMAS PUDDING.

¾-lb. McDougall's Self-Raising Flour.
½-lb. Suet. ½-lb. Raisins (stoned).
½-lb. Sultanas. 6-oz. Moist Sugar.
¼-lb. Mixed Peel. ¾ teaspoonful Salt.
Juice and Rind of 1 Lemon.
2 Eggs. 1½ gills Milk.

Proceed as for "RICH CHRISTMAS PUDDING."

Made with **McDougall's** *Patent Self-Raising* **Flour**

Early twentieth-century trade postcard promoting the McDougall's brand.

chalk powder to make it look white again. Some such additives were seriously poisonous; to produce what looked like Gloucester cheese, unscrupulous grocers were not above adding red lead to make cheaper cheese look the right colour.

The lack of simple hygiene was also disturbing. A sample of ice cream, analysed in London in 1881, was found to contain cotton fibres, straw, human and cat hairs, fleas, lice and bed bugs. Perhaps even more appalling, a chap called William Luby saw his boss making 'chocolate' by mixing brown paint with melted candle wax, and selling it to children; and even worse, he saw him buying sugar sweepings from the grocer's floor, seriously contaminated with dirt and spiders and peed on by cats and dogs, and boiling it down to make toffee!

This dreadful adulteration of food led to protests from the middle classes. They wanted to get what they paid for, and they wanted guarantees of quality. This led to the birth of the brand. The five McDougall brothers sold branded flour in Manchester, which became recognised for its quality. When they invented self-raising flour in 1864 they were on to a winner, and the company still flourishes. John Poulson took over a firm called Browns in 1840, won a Certificate of Merit at the Great Exhibition for his powder starch, and in 1854 started grinding up maize and selling cornflour. Luckily for him Mrs Beeton mentioned Brown & Poulson cornflour in her recipes, and he became a millionaire.

The five Gates brothers – Charles, Leonard, Bramwell, Ernest and Stanley – along with Bramwell's son Walter – sold various milk products and in 1885 had the bright idea of promoting their wares by using a picture of a cow (to represent the milk produce) and a gate for their name. The idea of Cow & Gate stuck, the logo became a brand, and the company is still going strong.

Even some of the more obscure brand names have survived. After several years of experimenting, coffee-lover Joel Owsley Cheek from Nashville, Tennessee, produced what he reckoned was the perfect blend of coffee in 1892. He went to the grandest hotel in town, the Maxwell House Hotel, and persuaded the management to let him make coffee for them – and so Maxwell House coffee was born.

These brand names were good for the successful manufacturers, because their products became more widely recognisable and saleable. They were also good for the consumers, because they provided both a guarantee of quality and a target for complaints if anything was substandard or went wrong. The same principles apply today, although many would say that the whole process of branding has gone too far: the sort of car you drive, the sort of clothes you wear and the sort of drink you ask for are important social statements, and in some cases the brand has even become more important than the product.

As well as brands, the Victorians loved to create icons, and the pursuit of progress was scarcely possible if you wore the wrong kind of hat. William Coke (pronounced Cook) became the first Earl of Leicester on the accession of Queen Victoria, and the family lived at the beautiful Holkham Hall in Norfolk. His son, also William Coke, was a great agriculturalist, but became worried about the estate's gamekeepers, whose heads he thought were in danger of damage from low-flying branches and aggressive poachers. To protect them he designed a tough hat, made of felt and stiffened with shellac. He took his design to the family hatters, Locks of No. 6 St James's Street in London's West End, and asked them to make him one. When he went back a week later to try it out he found that it fitted well, and also that it was strong enough for him to stand on, which suggested it would make good protection; so he ordered a dozen, and they charged him twelve shillings apiece.

The hats were a great success, and every gamekeeper at Holkham Hall

The bowler hat, designed for gamekeepers, became a status symbol for the upwardly mobile.

wears one to this day. To Locks it is a Coke hat, because it was ordered by Mr Coke, and a few people call it a billycock hat, in honour of its designer William Coke. However, Locks did not actually make the hats themselves; they sent the design out to a pair of hat-maker brothers in Southwark, William and James Bowler, and as a result most people call it a bowler hat. Although it was designed for gamekeepers, the hat was quickly adopted by bankers and engineers, and became the symbol of progress for the socially climbing middle-class Victorian.

For most ordinary people, however, life was less spacious and less gra-

cious. They lived several to one room in cramped houses with few facilities of any kind; they could not afford bowler hats or branded foods; and not until the Public Health Act of 1848 was there any real demand for proper lavatories. That Act said there should be some sanitary arrangement in every house in the country, and so started a revolution in hygiene.

COPING WITH SEWAGE

Today we complain that city streets are choked with traffic and we are choking with pollution, but Victorian streets were in some ways just as bad. Most of the vehicles – carts, trams, carriages and those 'gondolas of London' the Hansom cabs – were pulled by horses. In Oxford Street and Regent Street alone twenty-four tons of manure had to be cleaned up every day.

Even worse, though, was the problem of human sewage. Grand houses had water-closets and their own cess-pits, but most people relied on wooden seats over inadequate holes in the ground, in outside privies if they were lucky, but more often just in the cellar. The population of London rose from fewer than one million in 1800 to three million by 1855, and to six million by 1900. This dramatic rise meant considerable overcrowding and overloading of the system.

The sewage overflow from the cesspools and privies trickled through the inadequate drains down towards the river, accompanied by the contents of chamber-pots emptied into the street. The human waste in London was estimated at fifteen million cubic feet per day. The smell was indescribable. Worried about disease and death, the Victorians measured the smelliness of the atmosphere with 'eudiometers' which worked by igniting methane gas in a glass chamber.

THE GREAT STINK

Michael Faraday wrote to *The Times* on 7 July 1855 to say that the river was foul; he had taken a trip on a steam boat, where

> The appearance and the smell of the water forced themselves at once on my attention ... I tore up some white card into pieces, moistened them so as to make them sink easily, and then dropped some of these pieces into the water at every pier the boat came to; before they had sunk an inch they were indistinguishable, though the sun shone brightly at the time, and when the pieces fell edgeways the lower part was hidden from sight before the upper was under water ... The smell was very bad ... the whole river was for the time a real sewer.

The problem came to a head in the long hot summer of 1858. The sewage trickled into the river, floated down to Greenwich as the tide went out, and then slopped back up to Teddington ('tide-end town') when the tide came in again. Slowly it decomposed on the wide sloping mud banks, and the smell got worse and worse. The Houses of Parliament had just been built, and the members were tremendously proud of their brand new buildings; unfortunately, however, they could not breathe inside. All the curtains were drawn and soaked with chloride of lime to try and absorb the terrible smell. Goldsworthy Gurney, who was responsible for ventilation, wrote to the speaker that he could no longer be responsible for the health of the house. Eventually they debated the 'Great Stink' in Parliament, decided that something had to be done, and gave three million pounds to the Metropolitan Board of Works with instructions to sort out the sewage.

Joseph Bazalgette took on the enormous task, and designed and constructed five great intercepting sewers, three north of the river Thames and two south. They begin at Wimbledon and Acton in the west and at Hampstead in the north, run for a total of 82 miles, and can deal with four hundred million gallons a day. They were completed by about 1870, and ever since then, with the help of two extra sewers built about 1910, have been carrying all London's sewage way down river, to Beckton on the north bank and Crossness on the south. I had the privilege of inspecting the system at Wick Lane, where the northern high-level sewer carrying the posh sewage from Hampstead meets the mid-level sewer carrying the middle-class effluent from the BBC at White City, and from the inhabitants of Paddington and Oxford Street.

Climbing down a vertical iron ladder out of the sunlight into the darkness below was quite scary. The heavy waders were difficult on the ladder, but I was glad of them when I reached the bottom to find a knee-deep river of raw sewage. The floor was curved – the bottom of a 9-foot-diameter pipe – and uneven with gritty lumps of stuff I did not want to know about. The smell was not overpowering, but more than unpleasant, and the wealth of material floating on the surface demonstrated the extraordinary variety of things that people throw down the loo ... We waded upstream for perhaps a hundred yards to examine some of the original brickwork, for Wick Lane was where Bazalgette began building in January 1859. I was most impressed at the condition of the walls, which hardy seemed to have deteriorated in 140 years.

All the sewage moves under gravity, but because of the lie of the land

Sewage tunnels under construction at Wick Lane in 1859. Building the sewers of London was the biggest civil engineering project in the world at the time.

Bazalgette had to build pumping stations in strategic places to raise the sewage upwards so that it could carry on flowing downhill. Most of his building works were hidden away below ground, but when he had a chance to put up something that could be seen, Bazalgette really let himself go. The fabulous pumping stations at Crossness and Abbey Mills are fine examples of Victorian engineering construction – magnificent monuments to excrement! Crossness, with masses of elegant painted cast iron and four huge steam engines to lift the tons of sewage 12 feet – to raise it above high water level – is being restored and is open to the public. Meanwhile north of the river the low-level sewer that runs past the Houses of Parliament and along the embankment goes down to Abbey Mills.

There the palatial pumping station had eight steam engines to lift the sewage 42 feet out of the bottom of the Lea valley so that it could join the effluent from the other northern sewers, and carry on downhill to Beckton.

After the sewers were completed, there was no more great stink in London, but much more important there was no further outbreak of cholera or typhoid; the work of William Budd and John Snow (see p. 61) had at last been vindicated. In building the sewers, Bazalgette also engineered two other major changes: he changed the shape of the Thames in London, and he pioneered the use of Portland cement and concrete as a structural material.

In order to take his great sewers east along each side of the river, he had to place them as low as possible so that the sewage would always be flowing downhill, and this meant putting them on the river banks. To support and hide them he built the vast embankments that exist today. The Victoria Embankment on the north side of the river is perhaps most obvious just east of Embankment underground station, where there is a water gate now a hundred yards from the river. The Albert Embankment on the south side provides a fine walk from Westminster Bridge down past the London Eye and the Festival Hall complex. Bazalgette built these embankments by constructing walls at the bottom of the sloping mud banks at low tide, pumping the water out and then filling in the space with millions of tons of spoil and earth – a colossal undertaking. One result was to make the river narrower, and therefore faster-flowing, which helped to scour the banks.

Most of the sewers are built of bricks, but Bazalgette was innovative in the way they were laid together. Current practice was to lay bricks using lime mortar, but this hardens slowly, and will not set when it is wet, so instead Bazalgette turned to Portland cement to hold them together. Portland cement, invented by a Yorkshire bricklayer in 1824, had been used mainly for facing buildings, but Bazalgette was convinced that it would make a superb constructional material, because it sets hard even under water. Also he instructed his bricklayers to mix it with sharp sand instead of the normal soft sand, and to include gravel, so the mortar is actually made of concrete. You can still see the gravel between the bricks, and when repairs are needed, today's workmen find the old brickwork extremely hard to remove, with no sign of crumbling or decay.

Bazalgette also discovered that this concrete was both stronger and cheaper than bricks, and therefore used concrete on its own for some of the building work, including the embankments, which are mainly concrete

The Abbey Mills pumping station in the Lea Valley – a magnificent monument to excrement.

with granite facing. His assistant engineer John Grant was cautious and methodical in using what was essentially a new material, and rigorously tested every single batch to make sure it came up to specifications. In just a few years Bazalgette and Grant effectively turned Portland cement from a curiosity into the world's most important building material.

LAVATORIES

Before 1850 most people had minimal lavatorial facilities – privies out in the yard if they were lucky – although the rich might boast a Bramah water-closet and a cess-pit. However, as the middle class emerged they aspired to higher things, and they took advantage of the advent of real sewers and piped water to invest in their own personal water-closets.

To some extent this may have been triggered by the public lavatories installed at the Great Exhibition of 1851 (see p. 78), which sparked off two

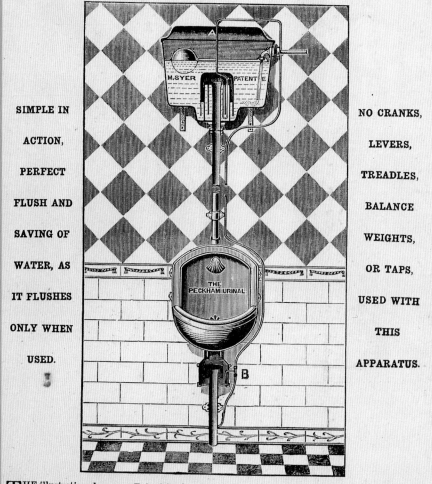

This automatic flushing system of 1889 is a direct descendant of the one patented by Joseph Adamson in 1853, and closely similar to the type used in pubs and other urinals today. The water trickles into the cistern continuously, and each time the water level is high enough to fill the siphon, it flushes.

trends. First the authorities realised that public lavatories were useful, and councils began to provide them. Second, people wanted their own at home. During the 1850s there was a rash of lavatorial patents. Before 1850 only about fifty had been taken out, starting in 1775, but hundreds appeared in the 1850s and 1860s, and the cascade continued until the end of the century. There were loos that flushed automatically when you stood up, loos that flushed when you pressed a foot-pedal, and loos with self-raising seats, but none of the thousands of 'improvements' patented later made a fundamental difference. The wash-out closet patented by George Jennings in 1852 – like the models most common today in continental Europe and the North America – and his wash-down closet of 1854 are extraordinarily like the ones we use in Britain today.

The one exception was the siphon, first patented by a Yorkshire plumber Joseph Adamson in 1853. He designed an automatic system for public urinals that need to be flushed say every twenty minutes, and he incorporated a siphon. The siphon has two considerable advantages: you get a splendid strong flush, and you cannot waste water. In the days before siphons people often used to leave their taps running to try and get rid of the mess, but once a siphon has flushed, the cistern is empty, the flush stops, and water cannot trickle away.

The water authorities felt somewhat threatened by the influx of water-closets. If everyone got hold of one of these fancy devices, and left the tap running, the reservoirs would run dry. So they latched on to this idea of the siphon, and in 1870 made it a condition of anyone fitting a water-closet that they should have such a 'water-waste preventer' in the cistern. This remained in force until the end of the millennium – British Standard 7357 (1990), echoing the 1870 Act, required that: 'Cisterns shall be supplied with an efficient flushing apparatus of the valveless siphonic type which prevents the waste of water.' Sadly this is no longer the case, since EU regulations allow us to dispense with the siphon and waste as much water as our European neighbours.

HENRY MOULE AND THE EARTH-CLOSETS

Despite all this water-closet progress, during the 1860s water-closets were almost superseded by earth-closets, mainly through the efforts of a Dorset vicar, Henry Moule (pronounced Mole). He took the living at Fordington, on the edge of Dorchester, in 1829, and although initially most unpopular with his flock because of his fiery evangelism and his determination to stamp out such dreadful practices as the local races, he earned their respect during the two great cholera outbreaks of 1849 and 1854. They say he and his wife Mary 'stood between the living and the dead', comforting the sick and dying, and boiling or burning the soiled bedclothes.

The revelation came to Moule as he knelt by the bedside of a dying man and felt, trickling past his knees, what turned out to be the overflow from the single privy shared by thirteen people, and he saw raw sewage bubbling up by the fireplace. He felt sorry for the plight of the poor, but he felt even more strongly about sanitation. After that hot summer of 1858 he decided that his cesspool was intolerable, and he instructed his family to use buckets instead of the water-closet. He began by burying the contents in a trench in the garden, and found to his surprise that within a few days all trace of the 'offensive matters' had disappeared.

He experimented, and discovered the benefits of dry earth, which seemed to absorb the smell and accelerate the decomposition of the sewage when they were mixed in the bucket; he wrote: 'The whole operation does not take a boy more than a quarter of an hour. *And within ten minutes after its completion neither the eye nor nose can perceive anything offensive*' (his italics). He brought in earth from the vicarage garden and dried it under the kitchen range, using it indoors in a wooden earth-closet that he designed, and patented in 1860. It's a simple wooden commode – essentially a seat over a bucket – with a mechanism for 'flushing' with a handful of dry earth from a hopper behind the seat, when you pull a handle.

In 1861 he produced a twenty-page pamphlet entitled *National health and wealth, instead of the disease, nuisance, expense, and waste, caused by cess-pools and water-drainage*. He asserted that 'the cess-pool and privy-vault are simply an unnatural abomination' – making the point that the sewage has to decompose somewhere, and the water-closet merely shifts the problem downstream. No, he said, the best way to deal with sewage was to use dry earth, which eliminated smells in the house and produced a luxuriant growth of vegetables in the garden. He quoted a biblical precedent, which is clear in the New English Bible: 'With your equipment you shall have a trowel, and when you squat outside, you shall scrape a hole with it and then turn and cover your excrement' (Deuteronomy 23: 13). But this was not entirely fair, since water-closets were not generally available when Deuteronomy was written.

Moule went on to write a string of tracts and pamphlets, including *The advantages of the dry earth system*, and *Manure for the million – a letter to the cottage gardeners of England*. He also tried hard to get government support, with an

1872 paper on *Town refuse – the remedy for local taxation*. He said that to supply mains water and sewers was fantastically expensive, and there was no need to provide public disposal. If everyone looked after their own there would be enormous saving in taxation and much less spread of disease.

He managed to convince a lot of people: 148 of his dry-earth closets were used by 2000 men at the Volunteer encampment at Wimbledon in 1868, without the slightest annoyance to sight or smell; 776 closets were used in Wakefield Prison; 500 went out to the army in India. In 1865 the Dorset County School at Dorchester changed from water-closets to earth-closets, eliminated smells and diarrhoea, and cut the annual maintenance costs from £3 to 50p! Lancaster Grammar School brought in earth-closets because the water-closets were always out of order 'by reason of marbles, Latin grammar covers, and other properties being thrown down them'. Moule earth-closets even crossed the Atlantic, and were made under licence in Hartford, Connecticut. I have made my own earth-closet, and used it for a month inside the house; not only does it work but the family were persuaded to try it out, and approved.

For some decades in the second half of the nineteenth century the earth-closet and the water-closet were in hot competition. Almost everything Moule said was true, and much the same arguments are used today by the champions of bio-loos and composting lavatories. The environmental considerations have not changed; whenever you use a water-closet, you not only throw away a useful bit of fertiliser, but you casually throw after it a couple of gallons of drinking water. What a waste! And flushing only shifts the problem downstream; the sewage has to decompose somewhere. Basically, Henry Moule was right.

As the world's population grows, that waste becomes less and less sustainable; if everyone in the world used water as extravagantly as we do in the West, the world's water supplies would probably run out in a few weeks. Switching to earth-closets would solve that problem at a stroke; we should

Henry Moule's earth-closet patented in 1860.

save a great deal of money by not needing sewage treatment plants, and we should all have a 'luxuriant growth of vegetables' in the garden. The drawback is that you have to collect the earth, dry it and every now and then take away the used earth and ideally bury it in the garden. This is definitely a bit of an effort, and decidedly difficult for all those living in city flats without access to gardens. Flushing a water-closet is much less trouble, which is no doubt why the water-closet won the competition for Victorian sewage, and why the plumbers were so successful. Even today we have heard of John Shanks and especially Thomas Crapper, whereas Henry Moule is forgotten, and the earth-closet, alas, is not among the many things bequeathed to us by the Victorians.

THOMAS CRAPPER

Thomas Crapper, born in Yorkshire in 1836 – the year before Victoria came to the throne – became a successful plumber and sanitary engineer. He set up his own business in London's Chelsea in 1861 and laid the

A Thomas Crapper design – it is coincidental that his name could also refer to someone using one of his appliances.

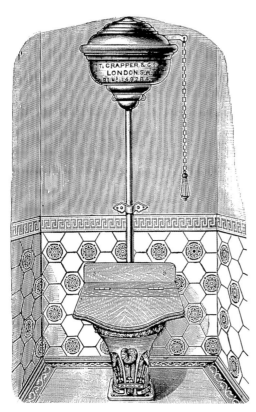

CRAPPER'S

Improved

Registered Ornamental

Flush-down W.C.

With New Design Cast-iron Syphon Water Waste Preventer.

No 518.

Improved Ornamental Flush-down W.C. Basin (Registered No. 145,823), Polished Mahogany Seat with flap, New Pattern 3-gallon Cast-iron Syphon Cistern (Rd. No. 149,284), Brass Flushing Pipe and Clips, and Pendant Pull, complete as shown ... ... £6 15 0 drains at Sandringham House in Norfolk when the royal family bought and refurbished it in the 1880s. You can find Thomas Crapper manhole covers not only at Sandringham and at Park House next door but also in Westminster Abbey and in many other places; there is even one in Bristol. However, contrary to popular belief, Thomas Crapper did not invent the water-closet, nor the flush, nor even the siphon. He took out a total of nine lavatorial patents for such things as improved drain connectors, but none of them represented an important invention. By the time he set up his company in 1861 all the important inventions had already been made. His was merely a successful business – it ran until 1960 and is running again today – and his name is a highly successful 'meme' (see p. 59)!

The word 'crap' meaning to defecate was in use in Britain from at least as early as 1846, when Thomas Crapper was only ten years old, so it does not come from his name. The word 'crapper' is used by some Americans to mean lavatory, and the story goes that American soldiers in Britain during the First World War were much amused by the name on many lavatory bowls and cisterns, and took the word home with them. However, even this seems to be untrue, since the first recorded use in writing of the word crapper meaning lavatory came some fourteen years later, in 1932.

THE WORKHOUSE

There had been various measures for helping the poor for a couple of hundred years, and the workhouse was a refuge where unfortunate people could live and work when there was nowhere else to go. Until 1834 they were fairly sympathetic places – above the door of one in Norfolk was the legend 'For the instruction of Youth, the Encouragement of Industry, the Relief of Want, the support of Old Age, and the Comfort of Infirmity and Pain'. The people who went there were generally too old or too ill to support themselves. Women who were pregnant and unmarried were often thrown out by their families, and the workhouse provided shelter. Nevertheless, for whatever reason you went in, the act of going there was like an admission of defeat and must have been traumatic.

The Poor Law Amendment Act of 1834 was a deliberate attempt to organise workhouses – there should be one in each parish, for example – and to deter from going there able-bodied people who should be able to find work without assistance. The conditions in the new workhouses were intended to be stark, tough and never better than those of 'an independent labourer of the lowest class', so that those who had the moral deter-

Dinner time at
the Marylebone
workhouse, 1900.

mination to better themselves would move out, or in other words fail the
'workhouse test'. The result was that many of those who did go to the
workhouse were elderly, sick or mentally ill, the people who did not care
about the spartan surroundings and the social degradation.

The Act included a highly controversial bastardy clause, which said
that until they were sixteen, illegitimate children were the sole responsibility of the mother, and if she were unable to support them, she would have
to go into the workhouse. This provoked an outcry and was amended ten
years later, when a mother was allowed to apply for maintenance from the
father.

The workhouses were severely criticised in the press, partly because of
the lurid stories of cruelty that emerged. In Rochester, for example, thir-

teen-year-old Elizabeth Danes was accused of leaving a little dirt in the corner of a room in the workhouse, whereupon the master, James Miles, made her lie on a table, took all her clothes off and beat her with a birch broom until blood came. Conditions were so harsh in the workhouse at Andover that inmates were seen to scavenge for decaying meat from the bones they were sent out to crush.

THE OPIATES OF THE MASSES

Providing proper sewers for all and workhouses for the poor suggested that everything was going well for people in Victorian Britain, but life is rarely as pleasant as the authorities would like us to believe. People have always wanted to escape from the grim reality of life by using mind-altering substances.

In the eighteenth century gin became the 'opiate of the masses', because it was easy to make and therefore cheap: 'drunk for a penny, dead drunk for twopence'. The name gin probably comes from the Dutch word *junever* meaning juniper (with which gin is flavoured), but in Victorian times it was commonly called 'mother's milk' or 'mother's ruin'. When the authorities first tried to curb the worst excesses with the Gin Acts there was great unrest, culminating in gin riots. However, the imposition of excise duty to raise the price, and the imposition of licenses for retailers, cut off the supply of cheap (and often poisonous) gin. In an effort to combat this attack on their trade the gin retailers began, from about 1830, to build glitzy 'gin palaces', which were large, imposing and elegantly furnished, with gas lamps lighting up shining brass, gleaming mirrors and buxom barmaids; according to Dickens, they were 'perfectly dazzling when contrasted with the darkness and dirt we have just left'.

In the second half of the nineteenth century distillers began to make unsweetened gin, which was called 'dry gin' and was much more palatable with the new-fangled American mixed drinks. This may have been the beginning of gin and tonic (see p. 85). Today the social strata have shifted, and gin – along with oysters – has become a favourite of the middle classes. Nevertheless, alcohol has always retained its appeal, and when Prime Minister William Gladstone brought in the Licensing Act of 1870, he lost the next election 'on a tide of gin and beer'.

Deprived of their cheap gin, many thousands turned to opium, which became freely available in Britain as a remedy for pain, coughs and diarrhoea. In 1797 Samuel Taylor Coleridge took opium to control a spot of dysentery, fell asleep in front of the fire, and when he woke up had in his head the whole of his long poem Kubla Khan:

> In Xanadu did Kubla Khan
> His stately pleasure dome decree,
> where Alph, the sacred river, ran
> Through caverns measureless to man,
> Down to a sunless sea...

Buying opium from chemists was easy: you could get a prescription from your doctor or simply buy over the counter a proprietary medicine containing opium. A doctor wrote in 1873 that he

> went into a chemist's shop; laid a penny on the counter. The chemist said –
> 'The best?' I nodded. He gave me a pill box and took up the penny;
> and so the purchase was completed without my having uttered a syllable.
> You offer your money, and get opium as a matter of course. This may show how familiar the custom is.

It has been estimated that in Victorian times five families out of six were using opium for medicinal purposes – even dosing their babies with it – and from there the step to recreational use was small. In some ways this was a step forward, since drink was regarded as unremittingly evil, the ultimate symbol of moral turpitude and degradation. Opium could be taken more discreetly, and did not produce aggression or violence.

Opium dens, as featured in Sherlock Holmes stories, appeared and flourished; there you could go and smoke in company. Many writers described the opium lifestyle – Oscar Wilde in *The Picture of Dorian Gray*, for example – and some of the bizarre images in Lewis Carroll's *Alice in Wonderland* are rumoured to have been inspired by opium-induced hallucinations. Those who disapproved blamed the opium dens on the Chinese, which was reasonable in San Francisco, where thousands of Chinese labourers had come over to work on the railroad in the 1850s and 1860s. They brought the habit with them and set up opium dens, which survived a prohibition law of 1875. However, in Britain it was almost certainly a myth. Indeed, the British were responsible for causing thousands of Chinese to become opium addicts.

The British had become great drinkers of tea, and before they set up tea plantations in India and Ceylon, they had to buy the tea from China. The Chinese demanded payment in silver for this tea, and for their highly prized silk; this was slowly but surely draining the British reserves. So the British East India Company started illegally smuggling opium into China from India and Turkey, where it was grown. The Chinese buyers were prepared to pay for the opium with silver, and the British traders then handed this back for the tea and the silk.

The Chinese authorities were determined to stamp out the smuggling, and wrote to Queen Victoria, asking her to stop the practice. There is no evidence that she ever saw the letter, but in any event the Chinese received no reply, and in 1839 they seized and burned twenty thousand large chests of opium, which represented about a year's supply. The British response was to send warships and declare war – a disgraceful piece of gunboat diplomacy. Defeated in 1842, the Chinese were eventually forced to open several ports for free trade, and to give Hong Kong to the British for a period of 150 years; the island was handed back in 1997. The opium wars of 1839–42 and 1856–7 have understandably soured Chinese relationships with the West ever since.

Opium smoking, as illustrated in 1872 by Gustave Doré for a scene in *The Mystery of Edwin Drood* by Charles Dickens.

PILLS, DRILLS AND DENTAL FRILLS

Despite the abuse of opium, there were some Victorian drugs that turned out to have immense and long-lasting value, none more so than aspirin. For thousands of years physicians had prescribed willow bark and meadowsweet for all manner of ills, and in 1763 Edward Stone, the vicar of Chipping Norton in Gloucestershire, wrote a paper for the Royal Society describing how willow bark in small beer or tea was a successful cure for fever.

Willow bark and meadowsweet contain natural chemicals called salicylates, which are the active ingredients. The problem is that they taste horrible, and indeed make you feel sick. Therefore the German pharmaceutical company Bayer decided to try varying the chemistry to see whether they could come up with an effective but less unpleasant formulation. Their brilliant chemist Arthur Eichengrun combined the raw salicylic acid with acetic acid (the acid in vinegar) to make acetyl salicylic acid, which turned out to have excellent properties in reducing both pain and fever.

The Bayer company tried to patent this new compound, but were not allowed to do so, because another company had by then started making it. So they played a clever trick. They invented a new name for it, 'Aspirin', and registered that as a trademark in March 1899. Then they sent out masses of promotional literature to doctors and pharmacists, praising this new wonder drug, and instructing the doctors to prescribe Aspirin specifically, rather than just acetyl salicylic acid. As a result they made a fortune, and the word aspirin entered the language.

What is astonishing about aspirin is that although it is not a natural compound it has a remarkable range of effects in the body. Not only does it reduce fever and pain, but it also lessens the risk of heart attack, stroke and some forms of cancer, and appears to have subtle effects in other diseases too. Apparently, if a thousand people in hospital were given aspirin, twenty-five who might otherwise have died would not do so as a direct result of aspirin, so wide are its effects. People over fifty who are being treated for many heart conditions, including high blood pressure, are now often advised to take half an aspirin a day.

There is a theory that people used to live mainly off manky old vegetables, which are rich in salicylates, and they provided protection against all manner of ills. Today, however, we eat only perfect supermarket vegetables, and as a result we lack salicylates, nature's protectors, and are more susceptible to disease than our grandparents, unless we take small doses of aspirin. Aspirin is now one of the most heavily researched and used of all drugs; it spawns some 3,500 papers every year, and something like a million million tablets have been swallowed in the last hundred years. So aspirin was one of the more amazing things that the Victorians did for us.

Perhaps less attractive for the patient was the first power-operated dentist's drill, which was driven by clockwork, and invented by George Fellows Harrington in June 1863. He manufactured them in his own factory in Ryde on the Isle of Wight, and sold them for six guineas. Twelve years later George F. Green of Kalamazoo, Michigan, came up with a battery-powered electric drill. After the arrival of anaesthetics in 1846 (see p. 63) dentistry became much more popular; for the first time people could have rotten teeth pulled out without having to suffer terrible pain. Many felt this was the answer to the problem of teeth that might go rotten, and they had all their teeth pulled out as a preventive measure; then they wanted false teeth.

To begin with, these were generally 'Waterloo teeth', real human teeth from dead bodies. Some of the corpses were indeed victims of the battle of Waterloo, but many were dug up by the grave-robbers or 'resurrection men' (see p. 67). These real teeth were set in hand-carved chunks of ivory from the jaws of hippos. They looked reasonable, although the bone-white 'gums' must have seemed bizarre, but the worst problem was that they decayed like normal teeth and therefore did not last long. A more embarrassing difficulty was that because they never fitted well they had to be held in place by springs pushing upper and lower sets apart, and occasionally these springs would catapult both sets out of the wearer's mouth.

False teeth improved greatly after the vulcanisation of rubber (see p. 121) led to the creation of vulcanite, which could be moulded to fit individual gums, made in a natural pink colour, fitted with realistic porcelain teeth that would not decay, and held in place under the palate by a suction pad. In much the same way the billiard table was transformed by the use of vulcanised rubber cushions which gave much better bounce than was possible before, and the invention of celluloid to make billiard balls saved the lives every year of 8,000 elephants which had previously been shot to provide the ivory.

So-called 'Waterloo teeth', real human teeth (supposedly from victims of the battle) set in ivory and used as false teeth.

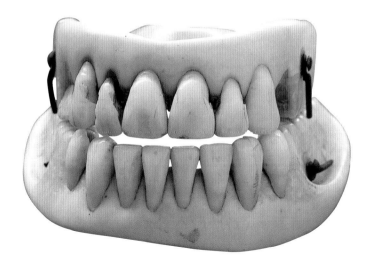

CHAPTER SIX

RULES OF THE GAME

THE VICTORIANS WERE great organisers. They saw themselves as in charge of things, created in God's image to control and manage, and to bring order out of chaos. In particular they applied rules to most of the activities of life – rules of conduct and behaviour, rules of war, rules of education, and rules of health and hygiene. They sometimes looked at each of life's events as a game, and they wanted to make the rules of the game.

Innocuously entitled *The Football Game*, this painting gives a good idea of the mob football of the time.

FOOTBALL

Football was played from the beginning of the nineteenth century, but in the early days it was rough and ready. The game might range the length and breadth of a village or town; there could be any number of players on each side, and play might go in and out of pubs and other buildings. Arms, legs and windows were often broken. This was mob football. At the same time the public schools saw games as an important part of education – not only character forming but also the ideal way to develop skills of leadership and teamwork. The Duke of Wellington implied that the strategies of war and team games were closely related when he allegedly said that the Battle of Waterloo was won on the playing fields of Eton.

Once the railways made it possible for teams to travel for matches, the organisers realised they had to impose some rules, so that both sides were actually playing the same game. The first attempt came at Cambridge University in 1848, when teams from several different schools turned up to play, but all with their own rules. In 1862 a set of ten rules was published and led to the Cambridge University Football Rules. On 26 October 1863 representatives of eleven football clubs met at the Freemasons' Tavern in London and agreed to form a football association 'for the purpose of settling a code of rules for the regulation of the game'.

After half a dozen meetings they eventually drew up a set of rules, which were roughly:

1. Size of pitch and goals (no crossbar).
2. Toss coin for choice of ends and kick-off.
3. After a goal, change ends, and new kick-off.
4. A goal is scored when the ball is kicked between the goalposts, at any height above the ground.
5. Throw-ins at right angles to touch-line.
6. No forward passing.
7. Free kick, when the ball crosses the goal line, to whichever side touches it first.
8. A player who catches the ball fairly on the first bounce gets a free kick.
9. No running while carrying the ball.
10. No hacking (i.e. kicking), tripping, or pushing the opponents.
11. No throwing the ball or passing with hands.
12. No player may pick the ball up from the ground.
13. No dangerous boots.

These rules were based on those of Harrow, Charterhouse and Westminster, and were not acceptable to all the clubs. Rugby school resigned because they disapproved of Rule 10 banning hacking. Their own brand, Rugby football or 'rugger', was developed by Blackheath football club into a game with rules rather different from 'Association football' or 'soccer'. Those first FA rules carry the seeds of today's rules, but the game must have been rather different without a crossbar, with handling of the ball allowed, but no forward passing, and with no rule about the number of players on each side, nor about the length of the game.

Some local rules persisted: Harrow rules did not allow handling of the ball, and there is a story that, when they played a visiting team, the Harrow players would present each of their opponents with a pair of white gloves and a pair of silver coins, which had to be held tightly throughout the game. This would clearly have made it more difficult to handle the ball. Around 1870 the FA rules were changed to ban handling. The first game under FA rules was played at Battersea Park on 9 January 1864. On 2 January 1865 Sheffield played Nottingham (later Notts County) in the first New Year fixture. The Football League was founded in 1888, as a ploy to guarantee more matches, even for those teams who

'The Rugby game as it is played at Rugby School', from the *Graphic*, 1870.

lost in early rounds of the knockout FA Cup. Preston North End won both the League and the FA Cup in the first season.

Gradually, between about 1850 and 1880, football changed from being a public-school game to one that appealed to the working classes. Most of those who joined the League were northern working men's clubs, some of which had been running for some time; the Sheffield club was formed on 24 October 1857. At the same time football was becoming a spectator sport; in 1873 a colossal crowd of 600 turned up to watch the match between Sheffield and Shropshire Wanderers. The custom of heading the ball seems to have started in the north; people laughed when this 'unnatural practice' spread to London in 1875. In 1878 the first games were played by electric light, although the lamps were sometimes uncooperative and plunged the pitch into darkness.

OTHER GAMES

In December 1873 Major Naylor-Leyland held a grand party at his home, Nantclwyd Hall, near Ruthin in north Wales. He offered his guests fishing, shooting, plays, a ball and several feasts. One of them, Walter Clopton

Wingfield, was so impressed by this event and the participants that he dedicated to 'the party assembled at Nantclwyd in December 1873' a new game he invented in the following year. He called it Sphairistikee, or Lawn Tennis.

Energetic young men in the 1860s could play rackets or royal ('real') tennis, if they could find a court, but there weren't many courts, and in any case these games were hardly suitable for ladies. Croquet was rather slow. Wingfield's game could be played anywhere with a lawn. He sold tennis sets, which contained everything you needed to make the court and play the game: poles, pegs, a mallet, the net, four tennis bats, a bag of balls, a brush and the 'book of the game'. The court could be assembled in minutes. No problem if the ground was icy: according to Wingfield, the

players could wear skates! The book was packed with helpful advice: 'Hit the ball gently, and look well before striking, so as to place it in a corner most remote from your adversary.'

In one year Wingfield sold a thousand tennis sets, and in 1877 the All England Club held its first championship at Wimbledon. Although Wingfield's court was dumbbell-shaped, with a short net and the court wider than the net at each end, the rules were standardised much more quickly than those of football, perhaps because tennis was a new and 'artificial' game, rather than one that had developed in various forms in many different places. Part of the reason for the rapid spread of tennis may have been the fact that young men and women could cavort and socialise together without breaking any of the delicate rules of behaviour.

Nuts and bolts

One young engineer who did break the rules of good behaviour was Joseph Whitworth, who eloped from Manchester to London with his girl-friend Frances Ankers. They went in secret by canal barge, which must have taken some time and presumably offered rather little privacy on the way. However, the trip had an important side-effect, for, having escaped to London, Whitworth needed a job and went to work for Henry Maudslay, the father of precision engineering. Under Maudslay's critical eye Whitworth then became obsessed with precision, and organised sets of rules for himself and other engineers to follow.

His most famous contribution was to standardise screw threads for nuts and bolts. General practice was to make each nut and bolt when it was needed, which meant that if you lost a nut you had to make another to fit the bolt. Whitworth saw that this was a terrible waste of time; if nuts and bolts came in standard sizes, then you could keep a stock of them, and they would be interchangeable.

He collected and measured nuts and bolts from several engineering firms, and then calculated an average shape. He settled on 55° for the angle of the V-shaped grooves of the thread, and on a particular number of turns per inch for each diameter of bolt – for example eight threads per inch for a one-inch bolt. He wrote a paper on his system in 1841, it was in general use by 1860, and was eventually accepted by the Board of Trade in 1880. Indeed, it was so successful that until about 1980 you could go into any hardware store or engineering workshop and find a 'half-inch Whitworth' nut and bolt. Thus in one of the simplest corners of the engineering world Joseph Whitworth introduced rules, and brought order out of chaos.

Whitworth's first paper, however, published in 1840, was even more fundamental, for it was all about how to make flat surfaces. He pointed out that 'all excellence in workmanship depended on the use of two plane surfaces' – in other words, if you didn't start with a flat surface, you could not make anything properly. He showed that the best way to make a flat metal surface was to scrape off any bumps rather than to try grinding, which was what most people did and just tended to make things worse. He would test for flatness by colouring one surface and then pressing it against a known flat surface to see where the colour came off – on the high spots. Then he scraped down the high spots, and repeated the process until the two surfaces fitted together perfectly. Realising that, even if two surfaces did fit together perfectly, one might be convex and the other concave, he insisted that three surfaces should all fit together, for then they must all be truly flat.

PRECISION ENGINEERING

Most engineers at the time were content to measure to a precision of a sixteenth of an inch, but not Whitworth: in 1856 he built a machine that could measure to a millionth of an inch. Others thought he was absurdly obsessed with precision, but he certainly prospered. He set up his own business in 1833 in Manchester, where Whitworth Street is named after him. He employed fifteen people the following year, nearly four hundred by 1854 and more than a thousand by 1880. This was a wonderful time to be making machine tools for other companies, since the railways were growing rapidly and constantly needing new parts, and the cotton industry was also taking off, with hundreds of steam-powered mills (see p. 22). Even as early as 1851 he won more awards than any other exhibitor at the Great Exhibition, and was internationally famous for the quality of his machine tools. Excellence was appreciated; rules were part of progress.

Whitworth was an important pioneer, but neither the first nor the only man to be fighting for standardisation of equipment. His early boss Henry Maudslay had built a production line of iron machine tools to make pulley blocks in Portsmouth for Marc Brunel in the early 1800s, and across the Atlantic Eli Whitney had at about the same time experimented with standardised parts when making guns for the federal government. He was followed by Samuel Colt, whose 1836 revolver with interchangeable mass-produced parts was one of the most important influences in the 'winning of the west' and created quite a stir at the Great Exhibition (see p. 78). Whitworth branched out from machine tools in various other directions: he patented a horse-drawn street-sweeper in 1842 and a knitting machine in 1846, and then when the Crimean War broke out in 1853 he began to make guns. During the next twenty-five years he took out twenty patents for guns, of which the most famous was the Whitworth rifle.

Most rifles had – and still have – a cylindrical bore, but Whitworth made his rifle with a hexagonal bore, and a hexagonal bullet to match. The hexagon spiralled up the barrel, making one turn in 20 inches, so that the long hexagonal bullet came out spinning rapidly. This gave it not only far greater accuracy than the Enfield rifle then in use but also, according to General Hay, four times the penetrating power at a range of 800 yards. The Whitworth rifle was a success, and even though for obscure reasons the British army refused to take it up, he sold more than 13,000, mainly to the French and the Americans. In the American civil

The Whitworth rifle and one of its hexagonal bullets.

war they became the favourite weapons of Confederate marksmen, who found that, fitted with telescopic sights, they were accurate at ranges of up to a mile. On 2 July 1860 Queen Victoria fired a Whitworth rifle during an accuracy demonstration at the National Rifle Association prize meeting at Wimbledon. She was delighted to hit the bull's eye, although she was helped by the fact that the rifle was clamped in a rest and pointed in precisely the right direction. In fact it hit the bull's-eye every time, regardless of who pulled the trigger.

One of the facets of Whitworth that delights me was his attention to detail with low technology: his nuts and bolts and flat surfaces, and the way he tested the effectiveness of the rifling of his guns. The war office paid for the construction of a shooting gallery in the grounds of his home, The Firs at Fallowfield, and he did his tests there. He mounted the rifle rigidly, pointing at the target. Then he hung up pieces of paper at regular intervals along the expected path of the bullet. After pulling the trigger he walked along the gallery, checking the holes in the pieces of paper. How precise was the path of the bullet? What was its trajectory?

Bill Curtis about
to fire a Whitworth
rifle on the same
rest set up for
Queen Victoria
on 2 July 1860.

Did it go in a straight line or did it veer about? Then, after marking each hole, he would fire again to see whether the rifle was consistent; in an ideal world the bullet would go through all the same holes.

THE SPEED OF SOUND

Along with precision in machine tools and firearms came precision in instruments; the Victorians were able to measure things more precisely than had been done before. Charles Vernon Boys determined the mass of the earth far more accurately than had been possible earlier, and also built a 'tele-thermometer' so sensitive that he claimed he could measure the temperature of the planet Jupiter.

The speed of sound was first measured in 1738 by two French scientists who took cannons to hilltops a few miles apart. When one fired his cannon the other watched for the flash, and then measured the time that passed before he heard the bang. Then he fired his own cannon, and the other man observed. By dividing the known distance by the time taken for the sound to travel from one to the other, they measured a speed close to the currently accepted value of 334 metres per second or 1,129 feet per second (in dry air at 20°C). The experiment relies on the fact that light travels much more quickly than sound, so that the flashes would be seen almost instantaneously. The point of measuring the speed in both directions and averaging the result was to compensate for any wind.

Sound also travels well through water; Leonardo da Vinci noted in 1490: 'If you cause your ship to stop and place the head of a long tube in the water and place the other end to your ear, you will hear ships at a great distance.' In 1826 Swiss physicist Daniel Colladon and French mathematician Charles Stum used Leonardo's idea to measure the speed of sound under water. They sat in separate boats, a few miles apart, on Lake Geneva. One rang a bell under water, at the same instant letting off a flash of gunpowder. The other watched for the flash, listened for the sound using a long tube sticking down into the water, and measured the time delay. They found that the speed of sound was nearly five times higher in water than in air.

The speed of light

Light travels about a million times faster than sound, so the time intervals are much too short for a stopwatch. The speed of light was first deduced by astronomers, who took advantage of the immense distances between the planets, so that the time intervals were easily measurable. The Dane, Ole Römer, working in Paris, noticed in 1676 that one of Jupiter's moons, Io, seemed to disappear behind the giant planet several minutes early at one time of the year and several minutes late six months later. This variation is caused by the time it takes for light to travel across the Earth's orbit, and Romer deduced that the speed of light was about 125,000 miles per second.

Measuring the speed of light directly is a tougher proposition; it needed ingenuity and Victorian high technology. The first people to succeed were French scientists Armand Fizeau and Jean Bernard Léon Foucault, in about 1850. They used slightly different methods, but based on the same idea.

Fizeau shone a beam of light at a distant mirror so that it was reflected straight back towards him. Just in front of the lamp he placed a toothed wheel, like a cogwheel with a hundred teeth, which he was able to spin at say a hundred revolutions every second. That meant that the light beam would pass through a gap between the teeth, reflect from the mirror, and then come back, but if it arrived back after exactly one ten thousandth of a second it would hit the next tooth, and fail to find a gap. So Fizeau merely had to increase the speed of his wheel until he could see no returning beam. Then, knowing the time taken for the wheel to turn by 'half a tooth' and the distance to the distant mirror and back, he could calculate the speed of light.

Léon Foucault demonstrating his pendulum at the Pantheon in Paris in 1851. As the pendulum swings to and fro in the same straight line relative to the stars, the earth turns slowly beneath it; so, compared to the floor, the pendulum's line of swing moves gradually clockwise (in the northern hemisphere) through the day.

Foucault also used a beam of light and a distant mirror, but he aimed his original beam at right angles, and reflected it from a rotating mirror close to the lamp. Each rotation of the mirror sent one pulse of light in the right direction to reflect from the distant mirror. As he rotated his mirror faster and faster, the returning beam hit it at a slightly different angle, and therefore reflected back not quite towards the lamp. From the rotation speed of the mirror and the difference between the angles he could calculate the speed of the light beam. Both Fizeau and Foucault measured the speed of light to be 186,000 miles a second.

Foucault also set up an elegant demonstration at the Great Exhibition. He hung a long pendulum from the roof and started it swinging north and south in the morning. As the day progressed the pendulum seemed to move around until it was swinging between north-east and south-west. In fact the pendulum keeps swinging in the same direction, relative to the stars, but the earth turns underneath it, so the pendulum's direction appears to veer round. This was a superb demonstration of the rotation of the earth, and must have provided a real thrill to those visitors unused to being confronted by pure science. A Foucault pendulum swings in the Science Museum in London to this day.

In 1877 a young Polish American physicist called Albert Michelson decided to repeat Foucault's experiment, but using a far greater path length. He set up his stationary mirror 9 miles away, up a river valley, and managed to measure the distance to an accuracy of a tenth of an inch. He measured the speed of light to be 186,355 miles per second, with an uncertainty of plus or minus 30 miles per second.

Light travelling at this speed takes just over eight minutes to reach us from the sun, but only one and a third seconds from the moon. The speed of light turns out to be a fundamental constant; it never changes even if it comes from a rapidly moving source. This curious fact was predicted mathematically by James Clerk Maxwell (see p. 130), professor of experimental physics at Cambridge University. Later, in 1905, it proved to be the foundation of Albert Einstein's theory of special relativity.

The periodic table

One of the most comprehensive applications of rules was the invention of the periodic table of the elements by the Russian scientist Dmitri Ivanovich Mendeleev in 1869. Elements are chemicals that are made of only one kind of atom, and cannot therefore be broken down chemically; carbon is an element and oxygen is an element, but carbon dioxide is a compound of carbon and oxygen. Even the ancient Greeks talked about the 'elements' – earth, air, fire and water – but by the nineteenth century the elements were being studied on a more scientific level. John Dalton had first proposed the idea of atomic weights in 1803, and since then scientists had been wrestling with the notion that there must be some pattern to the properties of the elements. For example the elements fluorine (atomic number 9, in order of increasing atomic weight) and chlorine (17) show similar properties, as do the elements lithium (3), sodium (11) and potassium (19). The British scientist John Newlands noticed in 1864 that these similar elements were often eight apart in atomic number, and called this a Law of Octaves.

Mendeleev, however, went much further. He made playing cards with the names of the elements on them and laid them out like a game of patience, trying again and again to establish the pattern, and he succeeded. The rare gases and several other elements had not been discovered then, so his pattern was incomplete, but he was so confident that he was on to a winner that he predicted that new elements would be found between calcium and titanium, and between zinc and arsenic. Sure enough, scandium was discovered in 1879, and gallium and germanium in 1875 and 1886 respectively, providing superb justification of his theory.

Nothing in science is so satisfying and positive as to use a theory to make predictions and then have them come true. Mendeleev's periodic table looked something like this:

hydrogen										
lithium	beryllium				boron	carbon	nitrogen	oxygen	fluorine
sodium	magnesium				aluminium	silicon	phosphorus	sulphur	chlorine
potassium	calcium	[scandium]	titanium*	*zinc	[gallium]	[germanium]	arsenic	selenium	bromine

Six more metallic elements in this space

This recognition of the true pattern of the elements was fundamental to the development of inorganic chemistry, and indeed of quantum mechanics and atomic structure. Without this periodic table as a platform, these steps into modern chemistry would hardly have been possible. Once again, rules had brought order out of chaos.

Statistics and Florence Nightingale

For some curious reason statistics became highly fashionable in the middle of the nineteenth century. A Belgian astronomer and statistician called Adolphe Quetelet latched on to this fashion, and published a mass of dubious statistics; among other things he invented a Law of the Flowering of Plants. Counting from the last frost, he said, common lilac flowers when the sum of the squares of the mean temperatures equals 4,264 square degrees Centigrade! This is complete nonsense, but Quetelet impressed many with his apparently mathematical reasoning. One person who was delighted with this statistical approach, and was keen to use it herself, was Florence Nightingale.

Her parents travelled a good deal, and named her after the town where she was born in Italy on 12 May 1820. Her father was a bookish gentleman, but her mother was a determined social climber, and cared only about who she and her daughters were seen with and where, and who they would marry. The younger daughter Frances was happy to practise flower-arranging, needlework and piano, but Florence was strong-willed, independent and rebellious, and wanted to help other people, especially in hospitals. Despite terrible rows with her mother, she went off and worked in a hospital in Egypt, and then in another in Germany.

When the Crimean war broke out in 1854, *The Times* sent W.H. Russell out to write about it; he was in effect the first war correspondent. He sent back blistering accounts of the incompetence of the army officers, and also tragic tales of the plight of the wounded. In particular he wrote that although the French hospitals were well organised, the English wounded were terribly neglected: 'Are there no devoted women among us able and willing to go forth to minister to the sick and suffering soldiers?' Florence Nightingale answered the call. On 14 October she wrote to the Secretary of State for War, volunteering her services. He wrote to her the same day; their letters crossed in the post. A week later she set off for the Crimea, with thirty-eight nurses.

Florence Nightingale.

In the hospital at Scutari she found appalling conditions. There were four miles of beds, all occupied, many by more than one patient. There were soldiers with wounds, soldiers with frostbite, soldiers with typhoid and other infectious diseases, all jumbled together. There was no proper sanitation, no hot water, no soap, no towels, no proper food. The worst thing was the disease; a thousand soldiers died of preventable disease before a shot was fired, and even at the height of the war seven soldiers were dying of disease for every one who died of wounds. She would not allow anyone to die alone if she could help it, and she sat and held the hands of 2,000 dying men.

She collected statistics on everything – the death rates, the admission rates, the temperature of the water, even the distance between the beds – and after she came back to England she presented her results to the Queen in the shape of what she called 'coxcombs', which were in effect the first pie charts. These showed how, once the terrible winter was over, the death rate came tumbling down, and after she had been there a year, the number of deaths from disease was only about equal to those from wounds. She was fiercely critical of the army and wrote in her report to the Royal Commission that the army took only the fittest young men, and every year managed to kill 1,500 of them through neglect, bad diet and disease. Those young men, she said, might as well be taken out on Salisbury Plain and shot!

Tough language like this was effective in getting through to those in authority. People began to listen to her, and so she managed to change the way that hospitals were run, and to change the status of nursing from a casual occupation for women fond of soldiers and drink to a caring and knowledgeable profession. She started a school for nurses, and wrote their first textbook. In other words, she applied rules in an area of life where they were badly needed.

Florence Nightingale was no scientist; she clung to the discredited miasmic theory of disease, and it seems that most of the improvements in practice at Scutari would probably have come about without her. Nevertheless, she was a tremendously forceful character, a catalyst for sweeping change and above all a heroine at a time when the country needed one. Also, she was humble. There was talk of her being buried in Westminster Abbey, but she would have none of it; she wanted to join the rest of the family in the graveyard of the tiny church at East Wellow, near Romsey in Hampshire. The family memorial is a smart square stone monument some ten yards from the church, with one side devoted to each of the family – father, mother and two daughters. The other three sides list their full names, spouses and achievements, but Florence's side does not even give her name; it shows only her dates, and her initials, F.N.

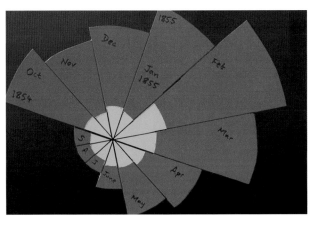

One of Florence Nightingale's 'coxcombs'. Each sector shows one month, starting with October 1854 in the upper left. The area of each sector in pink represents the number of soldiers who died of wounds; the area in green represents those who died of preventable disease.

RULES FOR EVERYDAY LIVING

The most famous of the Victorian housekeepers was Mrs Beeton. Isabella Mary Mayson was born in the City of London in 1836. As the eldest girl among twenty-one children, she spent a good deal of her teenage years helping to bring up her siblings. Not surprisingly she married, soon after her twentieth birthday, a publisher called Samuel Beeton, who had recently launched a twopenny monthly magazine called the *English Woman's Domestic Magazine*. Isabella soon became involved with the magazine, and later with its upmarket cousin *Queen*, launched in 1861. She contributed articles and became 'editress'. Her master stroke, however, was to collect the recipes sent in by readers, publish them in the magazine – after testing each one herself in her kitchen, she claimed – and then put them all together to form a book, which became *Beeton's Book of Household*

Management. This was issued in parts between 1859 and 1861, and then in an illustrated edition in 1861. The book was a runaway best-seller; it sold 60,000 copies in its first year and is still in print.

Mrs Beeton, alas, did not live to become rich – she died at the age of twenty-eight – but her book lived on, because it became the essential instruction manual for civilized domestic living. Not only did it offer meticulously organized recipes, alphabetically arranged, but it was also packed with more general social advice. She said that a people's 'way of taking their meals, as well as their way of treating women' were marks of civilization, and she provided careful instructions to allow her readers to thread their way through the minefield of etiquette. The new, upwardly mobile middle classes were ever keener to show that they were superior to their neighbours, and so concocted batteries of rules, about how to deal with servants, how to eat fish and how to lay out the knives and forks. These rules varied with the fashions of the year, and so in order to keep up with the Joneses you had to keep in touch with the latest trends.

Many people dined *à la Russe*, which meant extra tableware, since the table had to be laid with complete place settings: two large knives and a silver knife for fish, a tablespoon for soup – though this altered from year to year – three large forks and a silver fish fork, plus dessert spoons and small forks for pudding. (Mrs Beeton said that iced-tea spoons, orange spoons, and oyster forks were not strictly necessary.) The place settings should be two feet apart – this was Victoria's rule to provide enough elbow-room – and the cutlery should be a thumbnail's width from the edge of the table. The Victorians invented the table napkin, or serviette – a 28-inch square of damask, folded into elaborate forms – to wipe away any trace of food near the mouth. The courses were served by butler and footmen in silver dishes from the food on a mahogany sideboard.

Naturally many of the old habits became quite unacceptable: no member of polite society would any longer eat fish with just a fork and a crust of bread. All made dishes and most sweets should be eaten with a fork only. The knife should always be used for asparagus and salad, although placing a knife in the mouth would be an unpardonable offence against good breeding. And everyone should remember that 'the mouth should not be kept open in expectation of a well-laden fork's arrival, but should be opened only at the moment when it has reached the lips'. Mrs Beeton was precise in her instructions: 'The tablespoon is for consommé served in a soup plate. Dip the soup away from you, fill two-thirds full, and pour the soup between your lips silently from the side of the spoon, not the tip.' And later 'one old-fash-

A table properly laid, according to Mrs Beeton's *Household Management*, for a supper buffet in a ball room or an evening party.

ioned but unbreakable rule to remember: *Never leave a teaspoon standing in a cup. The instant it is out of your hand, it belongs in the saucer.*' However, Mrs Beeton is helpful rather than scolding about many social difficulties.

One of the fears expressed time and again in letters from readers is that of making a mistake in selecting the right table implements. As a matter of fact the choice of an implement is usually unimportant – a trifling detail which people of best position care nothing about. However, in order that you may make no mistake, you need merely remember that you are to take the outside – that is, the farthest from the plate   spoon or fork first. If the pieces have not been laid in this order, the fault is that of the person who set the table and not yours. If you are in doubt, wait until your host or hostess has picked up his or her implement and follow his or her lead.

These new rules provided guidance for the middle classes; many old aristocratic families ignored them, and for example went on eating fish with a fork and a piece of bread. An ordinary knife might rust after contact with the lemon juice often served with fish; to overcome this problem the socially climbing Victorians invented the flat, blunt, silver fish knife. So no member of an old family could have inherited fish knives; they did not exist in previous generations.

CHAPTER SEVEN

MAKING IT BIG

BEFORE THE NINETEENTH CENTURY there were essentially two classes: the rich, generally landowners; and the poor. However, the industrial revolution made it possible for anyone with enough drive and business acumen to acquire vast amounts of money, and these *nouveaux riches* began to form a new stratum of society.

A classic early example was Richard Arkwright, who invented and in 1769 patented a cotton-spinning machine. He had to borrow money to build his first mill at Cromford in Derbyshire in 1771, but when he died twenty years later he left a few mills, a castle, and half a million pounds. Although he became rapidly rich and bought a grand house just off the Strand, he failed to acquire many social graces and was never welcomed into London society. Carlyle described him as a 'gross, bagcheeked, pot-bellied Lancashire man with the air of painful reflection, yet of copious free digestion'. The castle he designed on the hillside close to his Cromford mill looks rather like a mill with turrets, and is curiously cramped and badly planned inside.

SELLING NEWSPAPERS

In Victorian times many more men made swift fortunes, and some managed to improve their social standing. Prevented from going to Oxford, William Henry Smith had to join his father's newsagent business, but then in 1851, against his father's wishes, he negotiated a monopoly of bookstalls on the platforms of the North-Western Railway. In 1862 he extended this to all the other major railway companies. The readership of newspapers was increasing rapidly, so the firm of W.H. Smith prospered, and he became rich. In 1868 he was elected MP for Westminster, and after he managed to prevent Mr Gladstone from building all over the Thames embankments, he was made First Lord of the Admiralty in 1877. The admirals would have pre-

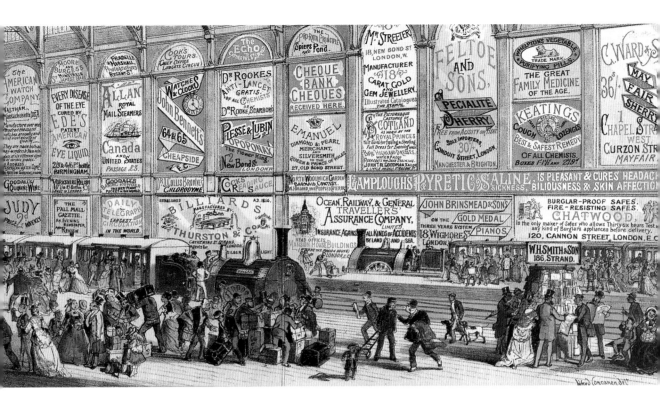

Charing Cross Station in 1874 with a W.H. Smith bookstall on the right.

ferred someone who knew something about the navy, but he did a splendid job of reforming the antiquated Admiralty. He also achieved the rather dubious honour in 1878 of being lampooned by Gilbert and Sullivan as the Rt. Hon. Sir Joseph Porter KCB in *HMS Pinafore*:

> When I was a lad I served a term
> As office boy to an attorney's firm.
> I cleaned the windows and I swept the floor,
> And I polished up the handle on the big front door.
> I polished up that handle so carefullee
> That now I am the Ruler of the Queen's Navee!
> Chorus: He polished, etc.
>
> I grew so rich that I was sent
> By a pocket borough into Parliament.
> I always voted at my party's call,
> And I never thought of thinking for myself at all.
> I thought so little, they rewarded me
> By making me the Ruler of the Queen's Navee!
> Chorus: He thought so little, etc.

COMPUTERS

Today we live in a world surrounded by computers, and it's hard to remember that personal computers have been with us for only about twenty-five years. Before that there were a few 'mainframes' in universities and large companies, and in the middle of the twentieth century the President of IBM, Thomas Watson, stated publicly that he thought the world market for computers would number about five – perhaps one in London, one in Manchester, one in New York and so on. Today many households must boast five computers, each of a power unimagined by Thomas Watson. The computers of today had their seeds planted in the nineteenth century by two remarkable men, Charles Babbage and George Boole, neither of whom profited much from their ideas.

Charles Babbage, born in London in 1791, studied mathematics at Cambridge, and before he was thirty years old he was elected a Fellow of the Royal Society and was giving maths lectures at the Royal Institution. The original idea of a calculating machine came to him while he was still at Cambridge, sitting in a library looking at a book of logarithms. He was lamenting the fact that books of tables always seemed to have errors in them, where people had made mistakes. In a flash of inspiration he saw that if the mathematical tables could be calculated by machine, there would be no possibility for error.

Because he was a mathematician, he knew that many mathematical functions have surprisingly simple 'differences'. For example, look at the squares of the first few whole numbers:

Number	0	1	2	3	4	5	6	7
Square	0	1	4	9	16	25	36	49
Difference		1	3	5	7	9	11	13
Difference			2	2	2	2	2	2

In principle, Babbage realised, the table of squares could be calculated not by multiplying numbers together, but simply by adding up the differences. What was more, he could imagine a machine that would add numbers together. If he could put together the right collection of handles and spindles and cogwheels, he could make a machine that would calculate squares, square roots, logarithms, sines, cosines – all the mathematical tables that anyone might want – and completely without errors. He called his machine the 'difference engine', because it worked from differences.

The difference engine as planned by Babbage but built by the Science Museum in London. The main section (behind) was completed in 1991, the bicentenary of his birth. The printer near left was finished in 2001.

He assembled the first prototype himself – a small model, with only six cogwheels – and showed it to the Royal Society, who strongly approved of what he was doing. He was awarded a gold medal by the Astronomical Society. Armed with this support, he persuaded the government to give him a large grant to develop a full-size difference engine. However, there was a hint in the negotiations with the Chancellor of the Exchequer of Babbage's incompetence. He originally asked for £1,500, and the Chancellor agreed, thinking that this was to be the entire cost of the machine. Babbage, on the other hand, regarded it as just the first instalment. Naturally the Chancellor was a little irritated when Babbage went back and asked for the second instalment. Amazingly, he eventually persuaded the government to give him the colossal sum of £17,000.

Babbage hired a brilliant engineer to build the machine – Joseph Clement had been one of the protégés of Henry Maudslay, father of precision engineering, and had his own workshop in Southwark. Unfortunately, Babbage told Clement to get on with it, and then went off for an extended foreign tour. When he came back he acquired a house in

Bloomsbury, in London's West End, and instructed Clement to move up there. Clement was unhappy about leaving his own workshop, and a dispute developed; who owned Clement's tools? Who owned the bits of machined brass that would eventually form the difference engine?

Money began to run short, partly because of Babbage's intransigent behaviour, and he went back to the government for more. They were not sympathetic; as one critic said, 'We got nothing for our £17,000 but Mr Babbage's grumblings – we should at least have had a clever toy for our money.' Furthermore he made everything worse by coming up with an even grander idea, which he called the 'analytical engine'.

The analytical engine was to have been a much more advanced machine. Instead of just blindly calculating one thing – say logarithms – it would be programmable. The idea was to feed it instructions, in what we would now call a computer program. There would be a store, where data could be collected, and a 'mill' where calculations would be carried out. Babbage was in fact describing a mechanical form of the modern computer. Unfortunately he had already blotted his copy-book. The government flatly refused him any more financial support, and the analytical engine was never even started. Indeed, we might not have heard of the idea had Babbage not inspired a young lady called Ada Lovelace.

Ada Lovelace was the daughter of the great romantic poet George Gordon, Lord Byron. She never saw her father again after her parents' noisy divorce in 1816, although he wrote about her in his poem *Childe Harold*:

Charles Babbage.

Is thy face like thy mother's, my fair child
Ada, sole daughter of my house and of my heart?
When last I saw thy young blue eyes they smiled,
And then we parted – not as now we part,
But with a hope.

Living in St James's Square, next to where the London Library is today, Ada Lovelace attached herself to Babbage, wrote a fine account of his analytical engine (translated from an article in French, but with extensive additions of her own), and described in detail how it would be used. No one knows how much of this was her work and how much came from Babbage, but she wrote down what were in effect the world's first computer programmes. She was tremendously ambitious, and hoped to work out the mathematics of the brain. At one point she wrote to Babbage: 'The more I study, the more irresistible do I feel my genius to be!' But alas she too, like her mentor, was slightly at odds with the real world. She ran up terrible debts, possibly because she was being blackmailed about an affair, and she died from cancer when she was only thirty-six.

Meanwhile Babbage too came to a somewhat sorry end. He seems to have become increasingly cantankerous, and in particular took against street musicians. He said he had had to spend a quarter of his life listening to appalling music in the street, and he managed to get an anti-busking bill through Parliament. This was not at all popular: people booed him in the street, threw dead cats at him and even paid musicians to go and play outside his house. After he died on 18 October 1871, only one carriage attended his funeral.

A VISION, IN A FIELD IN DONCASTER

George Boole's father was a shoemaker in Lincoln, incompetent enough to go bankrupt, so that as a teenager George had to give up his studies and go out to work in order to support the family. He could not find a job in Lincoln, so he walked 40 miles up the Great North Road to Doncaster, and became a teacher in Mr Heigham's Academy on South Parade. He hated his life there. He was miserably homesick, and wrote home lamenting the fact that no one in Doncaster made gooseberry pies as good as his mother's.

George Boole.

He loved to read, but had little money to buy books, so he deliberately chose books that were hard work and would take a long time to read, so that he would get maximum value for money. He found that maths textbooks were the worst, so he deliberately bought and struggled through them. This led to some trouble, for Mr Heigham's Academy was strictly religious, and Boole was accused of reading his maths books on Sundays and, even worse, of doing sums in his head during chapel!

One frosty January morning, George Boole went for a walk in Town Fields, just across the road from the school, and still a large green space in the centre of the town. As he walked there, he had what he later described as a vision, like Saul's on the road to Damascus. He knew that Newton's laws of motion explained the flights of cannonballs and the orbits of the planets; if ordinary algebra described the working of the physical world, could a different sort of algebra describe the working of the mental world? He thought, in fact, that he had solved the mystery of the human mind.

Well, he needed some years to work out all the implications of his idea, but eventually in 1854 he published a book called *An Investigation of the Laws of Thought.* He had not really cracked the mystery of the mind, but he had invented an entirely new kind of algebra, now called Boolean Algebra in his honour. It is a system of handling logical statements, and adding up a sequence of them to reach a final conclusion.

This work was highly regarded in its day, and Boole gained immense respect as a logician, but the real pay-off came almost a hundred years later, when British and American scientists were beginning to build the world's first electronic computers. The computers were effectively arrays of switches that could be off or on, which could be represented by 0 and 1. They needed to be able to add up the combinations of hundreds of these switches, and that is exactly what Boolean algebra was designed to do. So today, inside every computer, and calculator, and mobile phone, and microwave, is a load of software that depends entirely on Boolean algebra, the idea for which came originally to a teenage teacher, in a vision, in a field in Doncaster.

Bronze powder and steel

Henry Bessemer.

Fat cats became more common in the Victorian era because of the tremendous wealth generated in the second wave of the industrial revolution. Vast fortunes were made in cotton, in railways, in trade and in steel, and Henry Bessemer made several. His autobiography is a splendid tale of brilliant invention and skilful exploitation, and most of it was probably true.

He was born in 1813 at Hitchin in Hertfordshire, and after a couple of bright ideas that came to nothing, began to amass his first fortune in 1840, by making brass powder. His sister had painted several pictures of flowers, and asked him to write on the outside of her portfolio: 'STUDIES OF FLOWERS FROM NATURE BY MISS BESSEMER'. He decided to use his skill at calligraphy to write her name in gold. He was shocked at the price he had to pay for the 'bronze powder' – that is powdered brass – but when he realised that each ounce of brass powder cost more than two hundred times as much as an ounce of solid brass he saw the possibility of making a lot of money.

The price was so high because the brass was powdered laboriously by hand, and Bessemer decided to invent a machine to do the job. This turned out to be difficult, but eventually he succeeded and was ready to go into production. He did not patent the process, but simply kept it secret; he designed the production machine in five separate parts, and had each part made by a different company, with the result that no one but he knew what the whole thing was like. He had the parts delivered to a house he had bought near the old church behind St Pancras Station in London, and there he assembled the machine himself, fixing covers over each part so that no one who saw it would have a clear idea of how it worked.

The machine was powered by a steam engine from outside the building; the man who ran the steam engine had no access. Bessemer locked the house, and for thirty-five years the only people who went inside were he and his brothers-in-law. However, going in must have been a bit of a trial; he described the noise from one of the rooms as like 'the screech of a hundred discordant fiddles accompanied by the piercing screams of as many locomotives all bottled up in a small room'.

Nevertheless, this enterprise made him a great deal of money, which he used to finance more and grander schemes. In all he took out more than a hundred patents, including one for embossing velvet with specially heated rollers, and one for a machine to crush sugar cane – this in response to a challenge from Prince Albert – but he became seriously rich through steel.

Bessemer, like Armstrong (p. 190) and Whitworth (p. 164), had invented a rifling system to make artillery more powerful and more accurate, but this put extra strain on the gun barrels, and he began to look for a way to make better steel. Cast iron, containing about 4 per cent carbon, was cheap and strong, but brittle and liable to shatter if bashed with a hammer. The best steel was Huntsman steel, but this could be made in quantities of only about 25 kg at a time, and the process took three hours.

Bessemer devised a completely new method of getting rid of the carbon in the cast iron – by blowing air through it when it was molten, so that the carbon simply burned away. The first time he tried this out in practice he took a container the size of a large dustbin, half filled it with molten iron, and then started to pump air in at the bottom. For ten minutes nothing much happened, but then the blast of air 'sent up an ever-increasing stream of sparks and a voluminous white flame. Then followed a series of mild explosions, throwing molten slags and splashes of metal high into the air...' The reaction was so violent that no one could get

close enough to turn off the air, and for ten minutes the roofs of his neighbours were showered with red-hot debris.

When the reaction cooled down, Bessemer found he had just what he wanted – soft, malleable steel, ideal for casting but no longer brittle. The full-sized reactor vessel came to be called the Bessemer Converter, and he went into manufacture. Progress was not entirely simple, for although he announced his new process to the world with great enthusiasm on 13 August 1856 at the annual meeting of the British Association for the Advancement of Science, the steel manufacturers in Sheffield soon complained that it didn't work. The reason eventually became clear: their iron contained too much phosphorus, which fouled up the reaction, and Bessemer had to find ways of dealing with this problem. To begin with, he imported all his pig iron from Sweden, because Swedish iron was free of phosphorus, but later he developed the chemistry needed to cope with the phosphorus in the iron.

Then he set up his own steelworks in the heart of 'enemy' territory, in Sheffield, with his headquarters, Bessemer House, right opposite the works. The other steelmakers, at first highly sceptical, were soon convinced that the Bessemer process was the best. It yielded superb steel; it needed no fuel, because the reaction between the carbon and the oxygen in the air provided more than enough heat for the process; and it could make in half an hour a batch of at first five tons and later thirty tons, which was about five thousand times as fast as Huntsman steel could be made.

Now at last steel was available in large quantities at a reasonable price, and could therefore be used for railway lines, for bridges, for ships; it soon became the first choice of material for a wide variety of building jobs, and this consolidated the position of British industry. The Bessemer Steel Company made a loss in 1858 and 1859, but quickly went into the black, and in 1867 alone made a profit of £26,000. And apart from making his own steel, Bessemer encouraged other makers to make his steel under licence, charging them a royalty of a pound a ton, which was exceedingly profitable.

In his 380-page autobiography he scarcely mentions his wife and family, although the book is crammed with facts and figures about his brilliance as an inventor and his skill in business. He dismisses rivals with sarcastic comments, and for example pours scorn on Robert Mushet, who was struggling to develop manganese steel at the same time as Bessemer was developing his converter. In other words, Sir Henry Bessemer, as he became, was immensely sure of his own importance, superiority and infallibility.

A Bessemer converter in action in a German factory. The huge white flame comes from the vigorous reaction between the carbon in the molten iron and the oxygen in the air that is blown through it.

However, even Bessemer was not infallible, and he made one large and expensive mistake. He crossed the Channel several times and suffered dreadfully from seasickness; indeed, he wrote that

on a return voyage from Calais to Dover in the year 1868, the illness commencing at sea continued with great severity during my journey by rail to London, and for twelve hours after my arrival there. My doctor saw with apprehension the state I was in. He remained with me throughout the whole night, and eventually found it necessary to administer small doses of prussic acid, which gradually produced the desired effect, and I slowly recovered from this severe attack.

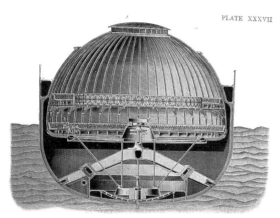

PLATE XXXVII

FIG. 81. SECTION THROUGH EARLY FORM OF BESSEMER SALOON, IN STILL WATER

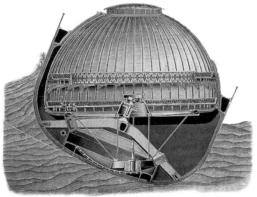

FIG. 82. SECTION THROUGH EARLY FORM OF BESSEMER SALOON, WITH VESSEL ROLLING

This sounds a fairly desperate remedy, and I can hardly believe that a doctor would prescribe a deadly poison as an antidote to seasickness, but that is what Bessemer claims.

His solution to the problem was typical of the 'can-do' Victorian attitude: Bessemer designed a ship in which he could not get seasick. She was to be very long – 350 feet – so that she would sit over three or four wave crests and not pitch up and down fore and aft. Then the whole of the luxurious cabin would be independently mounted on trunnions, or axle-like supports, with a huge weight underneath, so that however the ship rolled, the cabin would remain horizontal. Others were sceptical, but he built a full-scale model of the cabin in the field behind his house on Denmark Hill, and found that using a large steam engine to rock the supporting frame, up to 30 degrees and ten times a minute, the cabin could easily be kept horizontal. Then he went ahead and spent £40,000 building the ship, and launched the Bessemer Saloon Ship Company.

The *SS Bessemer* was designed so that the saloon would always remain horizontal even when the ship rolled.

The SS *Bessemer* sailed from Dover on her maiden voyage on 8 May 1875 in beautiful calm clear weather. She crossed the channel at a sedate pace and comprehensively demolished the pier at Calais, for the captain discovered that the ship was completely unsteerable because of the heavy mass swinging about amidships. The SS *Bessemer* never put to sea again, and the Bessemer Saloon Ship Company sank without trace.

THE *GREAT EASTERN*

The colossal *Great Eastern*, five times the size of any previous ship, in 1857. Surprisingly Brunel fitted her with paddle wheels.

By far the biggest ship built in the middle of the nineteenth century was the *Great Eastern*, Brunel's third and final venture into shipbuilding. Following his theory that ships became more efficient as they got bigger, he planned a true monster 692 feet long and displacing 28,000 tons, five times as much as any ship then in existence.

To do the actual building he hired John Scott Russell, an engineer with

experience of running his own steam carriage company and also of ship design. Russell owned a shipyard at Millwall on the Thames, which is where the *Great Eastern* was built. The whole construction was traumatic; several small companies went bankrupt, while Russell and Brunel had terrible rows; without Brunel's extraordinary determination the ship would never have been completed. She was too long to be launched in the usual way – stern first into the river – so they built her sideways, parallel to the bank, and had to launch her sideways, which proved extremely difficult and took several weeks. Then on one of her first trips, someone left a vital steam valve closed, and the pressure built up until there was an explosion, with horrific results: five men died. The strain of all this was too much for Brunel, who died six days later, on 15 September 1859, at the age of fifty-three. His friend and former employee Daniel Gooch wrote in his diary that Brunel had been 'bold in his plans but right. The commercial world thought him extravagant, but though he was so, great things are not done by those who sit and count the cost of every word and act.'

Brunel had built the *Great Eastern* big enough to carry 4,000 passengers and to steam all the way to Australia without refuelling, but in fact she was put on to the Atlantic run, and fitted out with luxurious cabins. At sea, however, she turned out to roll terribly, and on her first trans-Atlantic voyage she carried only thirty-six passengers. Her greatest triumph was in laying cables across the Atlantic in 1866 (see p. 100).

Going up

Traditional buildings at the start of Victoria's reign were made of brick, stone or occasionally wood. Any high building needed thick walls at the bottom to support the weight of the building. This limited the height of the building, since thicker and thicker walls at the bottom meant less and less usable space. Furthermore people were unwilling to walk upstairs for more than five or six floors. However, all that changed when two Victorian inventions came together: cheap steel and the lift, or elevator.

Once Bessemer steel became available in the late 1850s, architects realised they could design buildings with strong lightweight steel frames, and then simply hang the walls from them, in what has become known as curtain-wall construction. The first large building of this type was the Crystal Palace with its walls of glass (see p. 72), although its frame was of cast iron rather than steel.

In 1852 Elisha Graves Otis invented the safety elevator. Lifts or eleva-

Charles D.
Seeberger's
escalator won first
prize at the Paris
Exhibition of 1900
(see p. 190).

tors had been used for hundreds of years, for example to carry firewood to the top of the colossal lighthouse on the island of Pharos at Alexandria around 300 BC. However, most of the early lifts were supported by a single rope over a pulley; if that broke the lift plummeted to the ground, which made it rather risky. Otis's great advance was to install a safety system, which meant that if the rope broke, subsidiary support ropes or guide rails would take the weight of the lift, and an automatic brake would stop it falling. The first elevators of the E.G. Otis Company, which were steam powered, were used to carry freight, but he soon realised the potential for carrying passengers too, and in 1857 put a commercial passenger elevator in the Haughwort & Company department store in New York. By 1873 there were more than 2,000 elevators in action in the United States.

Using steel skeletons and elevators, architects began pushing upwards. The first true skyscraper was the nine-storey Home Insurance Building in Chicago, built in 1885. This building had water-powered hydraulic elevators, as pioneered some years earlier by William Armstrong (see next page). Hydraulic lifts were more reliable than those powered by steam engines, and are still used in buildings up to about ten floors; there are two elegant ones in the Science Museum in London. For the much higher buildings that came later, however, electric motors proved better, and they have been used since 1889.

The year 1899 saw one other new method of electrical elevation, the escalator, invented by Charles D. Seeberger and developed by the Otis Company. The name came from *scala* (Latin for 'stairs') and 'elevator', and the escalator won first prize at the Paris Exhibition of 1900. Sadly it seems unlikely that Queen Victoria ever rode on one.

CRANES AND GUNS

As the Victorians built more and bigger ships, and steadily increased trade with the expanding Empire, more and more goods were imported and exported through the ports. Newcastle-upon-Tyne grew with the business, and one man who profited mightily was William Armstrong. He was born in Newcastle on 26 November 1810, was well educated and trained as a lawyer, until one day in 1835 he had a life-changing experience.

While fishing in the river Dee in Dentdale, he watched an iron water-wheel that was being used to drive machinery at a marble quarry, and calculated that, of all the energy in the falling water, only about 5 per cent was being used and 95 per cent was wasted. He then became seriously interested in water-powered machines. He made a hydraulic motor in 1839, in 1845 he invented the hydraulic crane, and in 1847 he gave up the law to build a factory at Elswick, 2 miles up the Tyne from Newcastle, and to concentrate on his new business of making and selling hydraulic cranes. He was highly successful, and in the ninety years of operation the company made some 5,000 cranes. Armstrong also soon diversified, with such projects as the dock gates at Grimsby, powered by the water pressure from the specially built tower, 300 feet high. The Queen was immensely impressed by this and paid a jolly visit to see it in October 1854, laughing when her children were swished into the air on a hydraulic lift.

Hearing the news of the Crimean War that same year, Armstrong was appalled by the fact that the army was still using cast-iron cannons and cast-iron cannon balls. He was sure he could make better guns, and set out to use steel and wrought iron for the barrels, and elongated lead shells, with rifling to keep them flying straight. Rifling was not a new idea – Henry Bessemer, Sir George Cayley and Joseph Whitworth had all been trying it out – but Armstrong brought together several improvements, and within a few years produced breech-loading field artillery that was far better than anything previously available. Tests in August 1858 showed that Armstrong's guns were seven times as accurate as the previous weapon, and also had five times the range. His guns were accepted, he

Manufacturing artillery at William Armstrong's Elswick Works in 1887.

gave his patents to the government, and the next year he received a knighthood.

Armstrong's guns remained the best available, and his company went on making them, in ever-increasing variations, for some fifty years. The Elswick Works also branched into ship-building, and supplied complete warships to the British and other governments. By the time he died, eleven months after the Queen, Armstrong employed some 20,000 people. He stayed ahead of the competition by continual research and development, and throughout his life remained enthusiastic about scientific investigation. As he put it, 'However high we climb in the pursuit of knowledge we shall still see heights above us, and the more we extend our view, the more conscious we shall be of the immensity which lies beyond.'

During the 1860s Armstrong built himself a superb house, Cragside, in almost 3 square miles of gardens, landscaped from barren moorland, where he planted seven million trees. The magnificent house attracted magnificent guests, including the Shah of Persia, the King of Siam and the Prince and Princess of Wales, who were no doubt amazed and delighted by all the finest equipment and high-tech gadgets of the Victorian era. Cragside boasted not only hydraulic roasting spits in the kitchens and hydraulic lifts for the guests, but electricity – the first house in the country with electric power. A water turbine generated power for electric lighting, using first the rather inconvenient arc lamps (see p. 118), and then from 1880 the fancy new incandescent bulbs supplied by his friend Joseph Wilson Swan.

THE LIGHT FANTASTIC

Electric filament lamp (*c*.1880) made by Joseph Swan, who used carbon filaments made from synthetic fibres.

Swan was another successful entrepreneur, remembered chiefly for producing the first effective electric light bulb; electricity was being tamed. The intensely powerful arc lamp had been around since 1809, and was being used in lighthouses; for the stage, limelight was more satisfactory (see p. 119). However, these lights were too bright to be useful inside the house, so there was much discussion about the 'subdivision of the electric light', that is making less-bright lamps for domestic lighting.

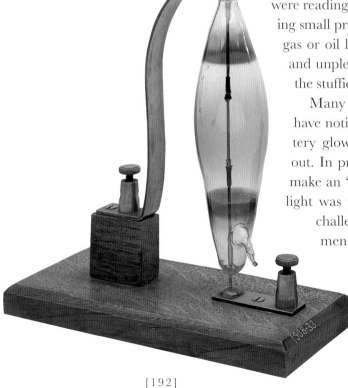

Victorians were becoming better educated and were reading more newspapers and books, but reading small print was difficult in the flickering light of gas or oil lamps. Also these lamps produced soot and unpleasant fumes, and the more there were, the stuffier the room became.

Many experimenters with electricity must have noticed that a wire connected across a battery glows brightly before melting or burning out. In principal they realised it was possible to make an 'incandescent' lamp – one in which the light was provided by a glowing filament. The challenge was to find a material for the filament that would glow without melting or burning. Today's incandescent bulbs have filaments of tungsten, but this metal is extremely difficult to handle and was not available to the experimenters of the 1880s.

The leaders in what became a race to subdivide the electric light were Joseph Wilson Swan and Thomas Alva Edison. Edison was one of the greatest inventors of all time; he had a team of researchers in his labs at Menlo Park, New Jersey, and produced the first phonograph (which developed into the record player) and the first practical moving-picture projector; he also had a hand in the telephone, and took out more than a thousand patents.

Having tried all the metals they could get hold of, both Swan and Edison had concluded that none was capable of standing up to the temperature they wanted – about 2,000°C. The best material seemed to be carbon, which does not melt below 3,500°, but they had to find how to make good filaments, and how to prevent them from burning, since red-hot carbon reacts readily with oxygen to form carbon dioxide.

The Edison electric filament lamp bulb, c.1880.

Both men concluded that they should put the filaments inside glass bulbs, and pump out the air, but that turned out to be not good enough; the filaments still burned away, because there was enough air 'adsorbed' on to the surface to support combustion when the filament glowed. The solution was to pump the air out of the bulb, switch on a small current – so that the air was driven off the warmed carbon surface – and keep pumping. This generated a really good, oxygen-free vacuum in the bulb, and the filament survived.

The trickiest problem, however, was making the carbon filaments. Edison was convinced that the answer lay in vegetable fibres, probably bamboo. He collected bamboo samples, stripped out fibres, and carefully carbonised them by cooking in an oven without oxygen. In search of the best fibres he sent men up the Orinoco River, up the Amazon, and deep into China and Japan; men died in the quest for Edison's perfect bamboo. Yet despite this prodigious effort, Edison failed to make a filament that worked. Even these tough bamboo filaments were uneven, and in use developed hot spots, which gradually weakened and eventually failed.

Joseph Swan had also tried vegetable fibres, both direct from plants and also carbonised paper – he even tried paper spread with syrup and treacle – but rejected them because of their inherent irregularity. Instead he worked out how to make artificial fibres from cellulose. He dissolved cotton wool or blotting paper in a solution of zinc chloride, and then squirted the liquid into alcohol, which made the cellulose precipitate as continuous fibre –

almost like a spider spinning part of its web. This fibre was homogeneous – all exactly the same thickness and composition – which meant that after it was carbonised there would be no hot spots or weak points.

Swan was proud of his artificial fibre, and persuaded his wife to crochet some of into doilies and other lacy things, but the real triumph came when he tried it in lamps. He carefully carbonised the cellulose, fitted the fragile carbon filament into bulbs, pumped out the air, applied the voltage – and it worked! The filaments glowed brightly and stayed bright, without burning out. Swan's artificial filament was made from fibres of pure cellulose – chemically almost identical to fibres of bamboo – and the carbonised filaments in the bulbs were pure carbon in both cases. The difference was entirely physical: Swan's artificial filaments were more durable because they were smooth and regular, while those made from bamboo always had irregularities that led to hot spots during use.

Swan first demonstrated his lamp in January 1879, and patented the pumping process, but did not bother to patent the lamp itself, since he knew that people had been experimenting with them for many years. Unfortunately Edison was more ambitious and had plans to light up whole cities. He announced in late 1878 that he had solved all the problems, and in October 1879 patented the carbon-filament lamp. Swan's response was to send a polite note to *Nature* saying that he had been making carbon-filament lamps for fifteen years, and in 1881 he began manufacturing and selling his bulbs. Edison threatened to sue Swan for infringing his patent, but his own bulb still didn't work, and eventually they joined forces, creating the Edison and Swan United Electric Light Company.

MAKE A BETTER MOUSETRAP

The Victorians loved their gadgets – the numbers of patents exploded during Victorian times – and one of the enduring symbols of gadgetry is the mousetrap. Wherever people have lived, from caves to skyscrapers, mice have lived with them, and dined on their leftovers; the art of mouse-removal must have occupied the minds of millions.

Colin Pullinger was the son of a carpenter in Selsea, and seems to have been multi-skilled: according to his trade card, he was, among many other things, accountant, builder, baker, undertaker, clock-cleaner, collector of taxes, cooper, farmer, fisherman, mender of glass, repairer of umbrellas, teacher of navigation, clerk to the Selsea Police and clerk to the Selsea

Sparrow Club. His sparrow-club duties cannot have been too onerous, though, for in due course he took over his dad's carpentry business, and around 1860 he invented a new mousetrap.

Most mousetraps today have a spring-loaded wire loop that is designed to snap down viciously on the neck of a mouse that touches the bait. This cannot be pleasant for the mouse, even if it is killed instantly, and once the trap is sprung it cannot catch another mouse until it is reset. Pullinger's 'perpetual' mousetrap was both humane, in that it did the mice no harm, and also permanently set.

The mouse was lured by the smell of cheese or other bait inside into the hole in the middle of the top of a narrow wooden box. Inside, its weight was enough to tip a cruciform rocker, which cut the mouse off from the entrance, so the only way out was forward, through a one-way mouse gate, into the main body of the trap. Meanwhile another mouse could enter the trap on

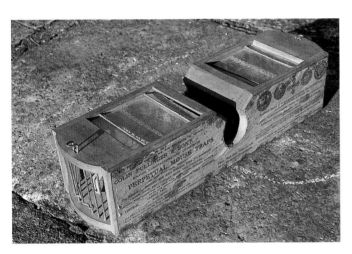

Colin Pullinger's perpetual mousetrap.

the other side of the rocker, and gradually more and more mice could accumulate. Pullinger claimed that he had caught twenty-eight mice in one trap in a single night, and also that a farmer had caught nearly a thousand mice in one trap in nine months. Presumably the idea was to release the mice somewhere else – perhaps in your neighbour's garden!

Pullinger's trap was immensely successful. He became the biggest employer in Selsea, with forty men and boys using horse-powered saws and drills to turn out a total of two million mousetraps, which only goes to show how right Ralph Waldo Emerson was when he wrote: 'If a man write a better book, preach a better sermon, or make a better mousetrap than his neighbour, tho' he build his house in the woods, the world will make a beaten path to his door.'

CHAPTER EIGHT

CRIME AND PUNISHMENT

DURING THE VICTORIAN ERA, the emerging middle class began to earn real money, and so to acquire property and material possessions. Increasingly they lived in cities, where they did not know their neighbours. They began to lock their doors at night and to worry about crime. As newspapers became more common and more widely read, everyone became more aware of crime. Indeed, they felt they were in danger of being swamped by a crime wave, although the actual crime rate was probably not changing much. The 1851 census identified 13,000 criminals and 7,000 prostitutes in London, but even if these figures represented a real increase in undesirables identified, it may have been caused only by the fact that there was for the first time an effective police force; the actual number of crimes may not have changed.

The Victorian policeman's uniform was designed to make him look like a servant with authority.

The same problem seems to apply today; our news media bombard us with dreadful stories all around the clock and all around the globe, and nervous people can easily convince themselves that burglars, muggers and murderers lurk round every corner. For the Victorians, however, this was a new and alarming state of affairs, and they wanted to do something about it.

LOCKS

The simplest way for the middle classes to keep their possessions safe from thieves was to invest in good locks. During the Victorian era Willenhall, on the edge of Wolverhampton, was the lock-making capital of the world. Two-thirds of the town's working population earned their living making locks, and there were hundreds of small firms of locksmiths, who made locks not just for Britain but for the Empire, exporting them across the globe. Many of these locks were simple, offering little security, but they were cheap, because they were mass-produced and made so quickly. In fact it was said (even if not strictly true) that if a lock-

smith dropped a lock he was making, it was quicker to make another than to bend down and pick it up.

Typical of the locks produced at Willenhall was the bar padlock, made by Richard Hodson and Sons and used to secure double doors, shutters and so on. This was a simple ward lock, mass-produced by hand, using simple tools and equipment. This type of lock offered limited security – any thief who knew what he was doing could pick it in thirty seconds – but it was enough to deter the casual snooper and was enormously successful; Hodson even exported hundreds of bar padlocks to South America.

The crowning glory of the locksmiths' craft was the Aubyn Trophy, an astonishing three-foot-high wedding cake of brass locks, constructed specially for the Great Exhibition of 1851. It was made with forty-four different locks, which were the most celebrated lock movements available in the country at the time. Each lock can still be locked and unlocked with its own key, but all forty-four can be locked or unlocked simultaneously with the huge and elegant Bramah key at the top. Among the large locks on the bottom tier is one by Pierce, which allegedly fires a small harpoon into the hand of anyone who tries to get into it – a sharp disincentive – and the Chubb recording lock, which informs the owner if someone has tried to pick it. The Queen commented on this lock when she saw it at the Great Exhibition, which no doubt did wonders for its sales.

The two major lock manufacturers, Chubb and Bramah, were enthusi-

A bar padlock from Willenhall, near Wolverhampton.

The Aubyn Trophy, a 'wedding cake' of brass locks produced for the Great Exhibition.

astic rivals. The Bramah lock with its curious turret-like key had been around since the turn of the century, while Jeremiah Chubb had started his company in 1813. They often used to try to pick one another's locks in order to demonstrate the superiority of their own, but in general these two makes were reckoned to be impregnable – until the arrival of Alfred Charles Hobbs.

Hobbs was an American who crossed the Atlantic to see the Great Exhibition, and while he was here managed to pick all the main locks. The Chubb took him only 25 minutes, while the Bramah took 51 hours, but nevertheless he got into them all, which was a nasty surprise. In practice the Chubb was adequately secure, and the Bramah effectively unpickable – how could a burglar spend 51 hours trying to get through your front door? Nevertheless, Alfred Hobbs's triumph really scared people. They wanted another option. Both Chubbs and Bramahs were hand-made and therefore expensive. What was needed was a cheaper option – a lock that was made by machine but still effectively unpickable. The answer was produced by another American, Linus Yale Jr, in the shape of a five-tumbler lock with a flat key. This lock was an immediate success, and to this day cylinder locks of the Yale type protect half the front doors in Britain.

The principle of the Yale lock was not new. To some extent Yale was using technology that had been developed by Bramah and Chubb, but the original idea came from wooden locks made in Egypt some four thousand years earlier. The Egyptian lock had a bolt that was prevented from sliding open by a number of pins that dropped into holes when the bolt was shut. Before the bolt could be slid open, each of the pins had to be lifted by exactly the right amount. This was done by inserting a wooden key with matching prongs, each cut to the correct length to lift its individual pin. Even if you were inside the door and knew how the lock worked this would have been difficult to pick, and the chances of making a key to fit were almost negligible.

The Bramah Lock Challenge

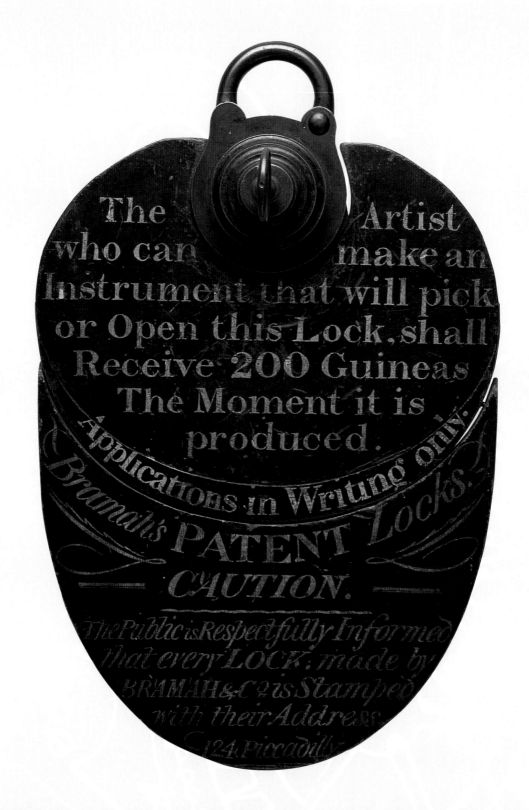

The Artist who can make an Instrument that will pick or Open this Lock, shall Receive 200 Guineas The Moment it is produced.

Applications in Writing only.

Bramah's PATENT Locks.

CAUTION.

The Public is Respectfully Informed that every LOCK made by BRAMAH & Cº is Stamped with their Address 124 Piccadilly.

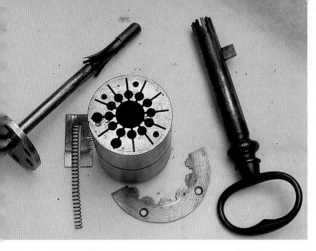

About 1801 Joseph Bramah, brilliant engineer and maker of luxurious lavatories and unpickable locks, displayed in the window of his shop at 124 Piccadilly an exhibition padlock mounted on a wooden board, with a challenge. He offered to pay 200 guineas – a lot of money in those days – to any artist who could produce an instrument to pick the lock.

The challenge was taken up fifty years later – long after Joseph Bramah had died – by the American locksmith Alfred Charles Hobbs, who came over for the Great Exhibition of 1851. Hobbs picked a Chubb Detector lock in 25 minutes, and then took on the Bramah. He finally got into it after a struggle that lasted 51 hours, spread over 16 days, all conducted in private, without witnesses. Bramahs paid him his 200 guineas, even though he had not 'produced an instrument', as stated in the challenge.

No one knows how Hobbs opened the lock, but we persuaded the Science Museum, where it has been on display for the last thirty years, to investigate. Accordingly their locks expert Keith Wilson carefully took the lock apart and examined it. He found a mechanism surprisingly simple and elegant, and beautifully machined. There is a theory that the lock was made by Bramah's foreman, the genius Henry Maudslay, although one internal brass part had clearly been given to an apprentice, since scrape marks show where the tool had 'chattered' across the surface.

Had Hobbs drilled into the lock to open it, and later patched up the hole? Keith could find no sign of any such hole. Nor could he find any marks of scratching or burring of the sliders, which

he would have expected if the lock had really been picked. Contemporary accounts speak of eighteen sliders in the lock, but when Keith opened it there were only twelve. Even more curious, these sliders were cut with false notches to make picking more difficult. These false notches were not introduced until 1817 – long after the original lock was made, as confirmed by Jeremy Bramah, current managing director of Bramah Security.

Keith (right) and Jeremy (left) came to the conclusion that the outer case of the Bramah challenge lock is probably original – and if so, Hobbs did not drill it – but the mechanism inside was probably replaced in the 1850s, after Hobbs had picked it, by one that was more up to date. Sadly, therefore, we shall probably never know how Hobbs opened that challenge lock.

The Yale lock used the same principle as the Egyptian lock, but with the bolt separate and the mechanism wrapped into a cylinder, like the Bramah lock. This allowed you to unlock the door from outside. Because the lock and key were all metal, they could be made to high precision – millimetres rather than centimetres – which meant that the key could be small and flat, and so would be easy to carry about and more convenient even than a Bramah. However, because Bramah locks were all made to order you could arrange for all your Bramah locks to be operated by the same key, so that you only ever had to carry one key in your pocket. Nevertheless, the Yale was the lock that swept the world.

Today's five-tumbler Yale lock has about twenty-five thousand usable combinations, so that the chance of one key fitting another lock is small. In the factory at Willenhall a pair of identical keys is made first, with a pattern chosen at random by computer, and then the lock is made to fit these particular keys. The pattern of one of the keys is read by a machine, which then chooses tumblers of the right length to fit into the barrel so that the finished lock will match that key.

POLICE

The origins of the organised forces of law and order lay in the middle of the eighteenth century, when Henry Fielding chose seven respectable householders and paid them to work together to prevent and detect crime. They were originally called 'Mr Fielding's men', and they quickly broke up a large gang of thieves, but were not popular. By the end of the century these men were known as the Bow Street Runners; they actively tried to catch criminals, but they did not have much coherent discipline, nor a uniform. Uniformed police appeared in Bow Street in 1805 – a fifty-two-man horse patrol armed with truncheons, handcuffs and pistols. Interestingly, even after the inauguration of the Metropolitan Police (see below) the Bow Street Runners remained the only detective force in the country, until they were absorbed into the Met in 1839; three years later ex-Runner Inspector Nicolas Pearce founded the Detective Branch.

Before 1800, however, police had been deployed on the river in London in an effort to control the lawlessness on the water. London was an immensely busy port, and the Thames was so crowded that as far upriver as the Tower of London it was often possible to walk from ship to ship across the river. All these ships were there to import or export cargo, and were therefore tempting targets for thieves, who employed all sorts of cunning tricks to deprive the merchants of their goods.

Hundreds of items were simply chucked overboard to be picked up by accomplices known as 'mudlarks', who would gather on the foreshore as the tide went down, ready to collect anything of value. Barrels of brandy were normally unloaded into small boats to be taken ashore, but unscrupulous boatmen might 'accidentally' drop a few barrels overboard for the mudlarks. Or might loosen the bung of a barrel or two in the boat, so that some of the contents leaked out into the bottom of the boat, and could be mopped up later.

The river police were set up in 1798 in order to combat this type of crime, and were arguably the world's first properly organised police force whose duties were all about crime prevention and detection, rather than political snooping. They set up thirty-five gangs, each of ten dockers, or 'lumpers'. The constables had lanterns, rattles and truncheons, and also swords and pistols or blunderbusses for protection. The lumpers had uniforms, which did not include pockets or the traditional dockers' aprons that had been vital for hiding stolen property.

Within the first year of operation the river police managed to secure convictions of more than 2,000 criminals, of whom two were hanged and 200 sent to gaol. Theft was so much reduced that the West India Company saved £150,000 over the previous year. In 1839 the river police were merged with the Metropolitan Police, and had to hand in their firearms, but got a uniform in exchange. They still operate today, from their headquarters by Wapping Old Steps, although river traffic is light these days, and they are more often concerned with general security and clearing flotsam than with arresting cargo thieves and smugglers.

Policemen in about 1850.

The Home Secretary, Robert Peel, decided there should be a similar body on land, and in the Metropolitan Police Act of 1829 created one modelled on the river police. He recruited 1,000 men to join the 400 already working; they were often called 'Bobbies' or 'Peelers' after him. They were based at Scotland Yard, given a uniform and paid sixteen shillings a week. Other towns set up their own forces in due course – Birmingham in 1839, for example – but it was not until 1862 that the government decided that every town in the country should have its own police force.

The early constables had a strict set of rules to follow, and a curious uniform to wear. Because they were the servants of the people – after all, the people paid their wages – they wore tailcoats, like servants. But they often had to take control and tell people what to do; so they wore top hats for authority, although in the early 1850s the top hats were replaced by slightly more practical helmets. The helmets offered a measure of protection from sticks and missiles, but more important, like the top hats, they added height and therefore visibility; even in a crowd you could see a policeman's helmet from some distance. Policing has always been mainly about preventing crime, and the very sight of a policeman is often enough to deter the potential villain and cheer up the nervous potential victim.

The man on the beat wore a heavy leather belt, from which were slung handcuffs, a light wooden truncheon and a vicious-looking cutlass in a scabbard. The cutlass was the ultimate deterrent, to be used only on direct orders from a superior officer when a line of policemen was facing a rioting mob, and even then never in anger but only in self-defence. In 1876 a Birmingham policeman called Sergeant Price was a little too enthusiastic in quelling a fight at Camp Hill, and sliced off the ear of a man who was attacking him. After that cutlasses were withdrawn from the men on the beat.

The job of the policeman on the beat was to walk a regular route at a steady pace of about two and a half miles an hour (hence the nickname P.C. Plod), and to meet his sergeant at certain fixed points in order to pass on any important observations – signs of unrest, minor incidents, barrow-boys selling things on the pavements, and even unswept streets; the constable risked a fine if he failed to report such things. He also inherited several of the jobs of the watchmen, and was often expected to light the street lamps, call out the time, watch out for fires and so on. He was required to help members of the public when asked, but was expressly forbidden to chat or gossip, especially to prostitutes, and was also banned from taking any refreshment in pubs or other such premises.

The day man was on the beat for fourteen hours without a break – from 7 a.m. until 9 p.m. – and even then he was required to stay in place until relieved by the man on night duty, who at least had a shorter shift. The constables were expected to carry food with them, and to get a drink of water from a public drinking fountain. The uniform was not particularly warm or waterproof, so in bad weather they would get extremely cold and wet. The policeman's lot was not always a happy one.

Each new constable was instructed to walk along the outside edge of the pavement, mainly in order to be seen as much as possible, but also to avoid being bumped by doors suddenly flung open, being jumped on from alleyways, and being dumped on by chamber-pots emptied out of upstairs windows. Each beat covered a fairly small area, so that the constable would become a familiar face in the neighbourhood, and as far as possible they were planned so that each constable was always within sight of another. This meant that if one of them got into trouble, perhaps being threatened by a group of roughnecks, his colleague would quickly be there to help. In case of serious problems the men also carried a rattle to summon help; this was changed around 1880 for a whistle, on which three short blasts were an urgent call for assistance.

The story goes that the police whistle, made by a Birmingham toolmaker called Joseph Hudson, has a tone inspired by an accident. He dropped his violin, and startled by the cacophonous clash of chords, realised that the weird noise could be useful, and modelled the sound of the whistle on it. The whistle was so effective and popular that it was soon issued to every force in the country.

Metropolitan police whistle.

In the early days the uniform had no pockets. This was because pockets can look untidy, and in any case the man on the beat had no need to carry anything – not even a notebook. If he was involved in an incident or arrested a suspect, then he was expected to remember the necessary information, and since the case would normally be heard the following day he did not have to remember for long, unless it was serious enough to go to the quarter sessions.

During the 1860s there was a technological leap forward in the identification of criminals, since the police forces acquired cameras, and were able to take mugshots of the villains, which for repeating offenders made identification far easier and more certain. Before then, all the villain had to do was move a few miles and change his name, and he could be confident that he would not be recognised by the local police. Once there was a rogues' gallery, however, there was a much better chance of sharing information.

DETECTION BY SCIENCE

By far the most famous of the Victorian detectives was Sherlock Holmes, with his Ulster cape, his deerstalker hat and his magnifying glass. Although he was a fictional character created by the writer Arthur Conan Doyle, to many people he was utterly real. Holmes's first case was *A Study in Scarlet*, published in 1887, and from then on he solved a string of criminal mysteries with a combination of cunning, science and logical deduction. Many of his best-known sayings remain clever and sensible statements: 'When you have eliminated the impossible, whatever remains,

Sherlock Holmes epitomised the Victorian interest in rational, scientific forms of crime detection.

however improbable, must be the truth.' 'It is a capital mistake to theorise before one has data. Insensibly one begins to twist facts to suit theories, instead of theories to suit facts.'

Meanwhile Holmes's scientific methods mirrored the developing system of forensic science. In India in 1856 Sir William Herschel began to use thumbprints instead of signatures on documents for people who could not read or write. In 1880 Scottish doctor Henry Faulds used fingerprints to eliminate an innocent suspect and to catch one of the criminals in a burglary in Tokyo. He wrote a paper for the scientific journal *Nature* explaining his ideas, and fingerprinting became a standard weapon in the police arsenal. At the same time forensic experts were beginning to make detailed examinations of bullets in order to show which had been fired from which gun. Chemistry was advancing too. By the early 1860s blood could be identified, so that even the tiniest spots on the clothing of a suspect became important evidence. The existence of separate human blood groups was discovered in 1900.

Poisoning, a popular method of murder, became more dangerous for the murderer after James Marsh, a Scottish chemist, discovered how to detect arsenic in 1836. Arsenic, or technically the white arsenious oxide, could be bought for poisoning rats, but was often used instead to poison husbands and wives. In France it was even called *poudre de succession*, or 'inheritance powder', because it was so often used to hasten the demise of unloved elderly relatives. The victim often experienced some gastric upset, but skilful administration over a longish period led to a death that appeared to be from natural causes, although a common symptom was a brown rash on the skin.

The Marsh test had two stages. First he treated a sample of body tissue with chemicals that reduced the arsenious oxide to a gas called arsine. Then he burned the escaping gas below a cold porcelain bowl, and black arsenic metal was deposited, rather as a candle will deposit soot on a cold saucer. This metallic arsenic is highly characteristic, and the test is exceedingly sensitive; traces of arsenic can be found in the body of a poison victim months after the death. Therefore when arsenic poisoning was suspected, proving it was no longer a problem. In the celebrated case of Charles Lafarge, who was poisoned with arsenic in 1840, his body was exhumed, the Marsh test applied, and his wife Marie, who had recently bought rat poison, was convicted of murder.

THE CRIMINALS

Meanwhile, what of the villains, the cause of the fear and anxiety? They were thieves, pickpockets, forgers, confidence tricksters and occasionally murderers. They came from all sectors of society; some of the thieves were merely boys who pinched apples from barrows, while 'Jem the Penman', who relieved the Bank of England of £100,000 in 1873 turned out to be a barrister of the Inner Temple. Many of the criminals were highly professional; they had their safe-cracking tools made to order by the finest craftsmen in Birmingham and Sheffield.

At the West Midlands Police Museum they have records of all the cases since the force arrived in 1839, and the details are fascinating. In 1860, for example, a pair of brothers aged sixteen and eighteen were sentenced to eighteen months in gaol for 'base coin' – that is for making counterfeit coins – and a chap called Gray, alias Murphy, was sentenced to ten years in prison for stealing a rabbit! One can only guess that he had been convicted of other crimes in the past, and that he was given such a severe sentence partly as a result of his previous record. Corporal punishment was common – six strokes of the birch each for a pair of teenage boys who stole thirty shillings, and a severe flogging for an attempted garrotting.

However, the sentences were becoming more lenient. In 1800 you could be hanged or deported for more than 160 different crimes, even for some trivial thefts – you 'might as well be hanged for a sheep as for a

The rogues' gallery was a big step forward in identification of criminals, especially repeating offenders.

lamb'. After becoming Home Secretary in 1822, Robert Peel began the task of abolishing the 'Bloody Code', and by the time Victoria became queen you could be hanged only for murder or treason. Deportation was abandoned in the 1850s and 1860s. The new Victorian penal system was generally less harsh than what had gone before.

FORGERY

This new more lenient attitude had the effect of broadening the criminal horizons; now that the penalty was only a gaol sentence, it became well worth taking the risk of perpetrating such minor crimes as forgery. The first printed banknotes were issued only in 1855, and for some decades most people never came into contact with notes; so most early Victorian forgery was of coins, and the offence was often known as 'base coin'.

One common trick used to defraud shopkeepers was known as 'ringing the changes'. The criminal goes into a shop pretending to be a customer, and asks for a small item, perhaps a handkerchief, offering a sovereign in payment. The shopkeeper bounces it on the glass counter, knowing that a genuine sovereign 'rings' when bounced, whereas a counterfeit one does not ring true – and the sovereign does indeed ring, it is true. At that moment the 'customer' says that he thinks he may have some smaller change, takes back the sovereign and fumbles in his pockets. Then he says apologetically that he must have been mistaken, hands back the sovereign and takes his handkerchief and the change. What the shopkeeper has failed to notice is that the second sovereign is not the same as the first. The 'customer' has switched the genuine coin for a forged one by sleight of hand, and so gets a handkerchief and change for a sovereign for his worthless piece of metal.

Making a fake gold coin by electroplating.

Many metalworkers had access to the technology necessary for casting or stamping metals into roughly the right shapes to be passed off as coins; the tricky part was getting them to look the right colour, and feel roughly the right weight. This was where science came to the aid of the criminal.

By the 1850s good batteries were available, and would supply a steady and reliable current. Meanwhile chemists had found out how to deposit gold from solution, in other words how to make gold plate. There are suggestions that people discovered electroplating hundreds of years earlier, in what is now Iraq or even in ancient Egypt, possibly using chemicals that are by-products of leather tanning. However, the 'modern' way to electroplate with gold is to deposit the gold from a solution of potassium gold cyanide. The anode today might be an expensive piece of platinised aluminium, but the Victorians would have used gold in a slightly less efficient process.

The fake metal coin is the cathode, suspended on a piece of copper wire. Gold is dense (19 grams per cubic centimetre), so the forgers had to use as dense a metal as possible to avoid alerting anyone. Lead is dense (13 grams per cubic centimetre) but does not electroplate well, so the forgers often used silver or platinum. Ironically, however, the price of platinum rose sharply until it was higher than that of gold, which meant that the criminals had to stop using it, or they would be losing money on every sovereign they made. Electroplating releases some fine bubbles of hydrogen gas and deposits a very thin layer of gold evenly on the metal surface without leaving any gaps or holes, so that from the outside it is impossible to tell whether the object is plated or pure gold.

Once the criminals had latched on to science like this, the fake sovereigns became hard to spot, and the best check was by weight. Gentlemen, therefore, relied on science too; they used to carry a miniature balance with which they could check the weight of the coin and see at once whether it was genuine.

MURDER

The most notorious criminal in Victorian Britain was Jack the Ripper, who murdered several prostitutes in the Whitechapel area of East London in 1888. So much has been written about the Whitechapel murders that disentangling fact from fancy is now difficult, and no one was ever convicted of the crimes.

The police were fairly certain that one man was responsible for murdering Mary Ann Nichols at 3.40 a.m. on Friday 31 August, Annie Chapman early in the morning of Saturday 8 September, Elizabeth Stride at 1 a.m. on Saturday 30 September, Catherine Eddowes about an hour later on the same night, and Mary Jane Kelly around 4 a.m. on Friday 9 November. Two earlier murders and four later ones have also been attributed to the same man, but these cases are more doubtful.

Of the five sure victims, Elizabeth Stride had only just had her throat cut when her body was found, and it seemed that the murderer was disturbed – a cab driver almost caught him in the act. The other four all had their throats cut and were horribly mutilated, and there was some evidence that the killer had anatomical knowledge.

On 27 September 1888 the Central News Agency received a lurid letter which began 'Dear Boss,' continued with sentences like 'I am down on whores and I shant quit ripping them till I do get buckled', and was signed 'Yours truly Jack the Ripper'. A postcard, apparently from the same man, was posted on 1 October, boasting about the two murders of 30 September.

The police were severely criticised for their handling of the case. They put extra men on the beat and set up stake-outs, without success. They asked a police surgeon to look at the victims to try to establish what had happened. They even brought in a pair of bloodhounds to try and track the villain down, but while the dogs were in London there were no more murders, and the police decided their food was costing too much, and sent them home.

Dozens of candidates have been suggested as the real Jack the Ripper,

POLICE · BUDGET · EDITION

EDITED · BY · HAROLD · FURNISS

FAMOUS CRIMES

PAST · AND · PRESENT

ONE · PENNY

THE DISCOVERY OF "JACK THE RIPPER'S" FIRST MURDER.

Vol. II.—No. 15.

The horrifying saga of Jack the Ripper provided ideal copy for the lurid magazines known as 'penny dreadfuls'.

but the police eventually settled on four main suspects: a Polish Jew called Kosminski, a barrister and teacher called John Druitt, a Russian thief and con-man called Michael Ostrog, and an American 'quack' doctor called Francis Tumblety. Druitt committed suicide in December 1888. Tumblety probably had the necessary anatomical knowledge; he was arrested in November 1888 for gross indecency, but jumped bail and fled the country. Ostrog was arrested, and had spent some time in asylums. However, the police never had any hard evidence against any of the four, and the Whitechapel murders remain unsolved.

The Victorians were already scared about crime, and these Whitechapel murders touched a raw nerve. The Queen wrote to the Home Secretary expressing her concern, and the people were desperate to find out all they could, so newspapers were only too happy to print all the lurid details. Some people even suggested that a few unscrupulous journalists planted false evidence in order to get their own exclusives, and to keep the story on the boil.

Another murderous tale involved Mary Ann Cotton, who lost four husbands and a dozen children in what at first seemed a series of natural tragedies. She first married in 1844, when she was twenty-two, and with her husband William had five children, who all mysteriously died in infancy of 'gastric fever'. Then in 1865 William too died of 'gastric fever'. She became a junior nurse, and had access to a hospital supply of arsenic. She married again, and her second husband died fifteen months later; like her first husband, he had insured his life.

She married John Robinson, who had five children, three of whom died in the following year – of 'gastric fever'. Then she ran away with a number of his valuables; he was lucky. Mary Ann went to look after her ageing mother, who strangely died, quite soon, of 'gastric fever'. Mary went to Newcastle and married a rich widower, Frederick Cotton, but he died, along with their child, three of his children, a boarder and several pigs.

Finally a local doctor became suspicious, and the Marsh test showed that there was enough arsenic in the latest victim, a little boy called Charles, to kill five people. Mary Ann Cotton, having killed probably twenty-one people, was hanged at Durham County Gaol on 24 March 1873.

THE LONG DROP

Speaking of hanging, there was a dramatic change in methods around 1875, introduced by William Marwood, a cobbler in Horncastle. He thought that the normal system of hanging was inhumane, because the victim was simply suspended by a noose around the neck, and choked to death by suffocation, which often took ten minutes even if the victim's family and friends went and pulled down on the legs to increase the pressure and decrease the time of agony. So Marwood introduced the concept of the 'long drop'. He realised that if the customer dropped a few feet and was brought up short by the rope, the sudden jerk would break the neck and cause instant death.

More precisely, if the hangman's knot was tucked tight under the corner of the jaw just in front of the left ear, then the right upward jerk by the rope caused a fracture dislocation of the atlanto-axial junction between the second and third vertebrae, which severed the spinal cord and so caused instant brain death. You can feel the atlanto-axial junction for yourself: put your fingers on the back of your neck as you turn your head left and right. The vertebrae are the hard knobs of bone. Your backbone feels fairly rigid, and the highest lump on it is the third vertebra; the one above it – the first one that moves as you turn your neck – is the second vertebra. The gap between them is where your neck would break. The tricky bit was working out the optimal length of the drop; Marwood did calculations based on the weight of the victim and the thickness of the neck, in order to cause instant death without pulling the head off.

So in Marwood's regime the execution victim, hands tied behind the back, was led up on to a scaffold and stood on a trap door. The noose was fastened around the neck, a priest would pray for the victim's soul, a black bag would be pulled over the head, and finally the trap door was opened, and the victim fell perhaps seven or eight feet before coming to the end of the rope. Marwood boasted of his advances over his rivals: 'They hang 'em; I execute 'em!' He was proud of his work; people came from far afield to meet him, and he used to sell his bootlaces at double the normal price, because he was the hangman.

PRISONS

The introduction of an efficient police force and the development of forensic science led to the conviction of increasing numbers of criminals, which meant that the Victorians had to build new prisons to accommodate them. Many of today's gaols are Victorian, including Armley Gaol in Leeds, Winson Green in Birmingham, Strangeways in Manchester and Wormwood Scrubs close to the BBC in West London.

A Victorian prison cell, designed for solitude.

Before the Victorian era prisons were more like dens of iniquity than houses of correction. Most prisoners had access to gin shops and prostitutes, and indeed your time as a prisoner depended on how rich you were. Prisoners had to pay their gaolers, so prisoners who paid more got better treatment. Those who could afford it might lodge in the governor's house, and it was even possible to pay someone else to serve your sentence for you! After a visit to the Newgate Prison in 1836, inspectors, horrified at finding men so drunk they could not even sit upright, let alone stand, reported their findings: they saw 'a body of criminals of every class in riot, debauchery and gaming'. The inspectors' report shocked Parliament and the nation. Regardless of expense, a new penal system had to be developed – a system dedicated to moral regeneration.

The large new prisons that were built as a result of these reforms are the ones we still use today. The architecture tended to follow a pattern of a warders' area in the centre, with wings going off in each direction, in either a cross or a star shape, so that warders could watch prisoners on every wing. Unfortunately, what the architects had not foreseen was that the prisoners stared back at the warders, and according to some accounts drove them mad.

The regime inside these new prisons was designed to be one of punishment. The authorities wanted to get right away from the debauchery of Newgate, so they went for 'solitude and servitude'. Solitude meant isolation; even in a crowded prison, prisoners weren't allowed to talk to each other. They had to wear leather Scotch caps pulled down to hide their faces, so that they could not be recognised; they were identifiable only by a number sewn on their otherwise anonymous uniforms.

Servitude meant hard work, and the inmates were made to perform a range of tasks, most of which were mind-numbing in their futility. Shot drill meant carrying a pile of heavy cannon balls one by one across the prison yard, and then back again. After an hour and a half of this the prisoners felt suitably punished. Perhaps even more pointless was the crank. The prisoner had to turn a crank handle 10,000 times in an eight-hour day – that's 1,200 times an hour, or once every three seconds. There was absolutely no point to it – no useful work was done – but occasionally an officer would come along and tighten the handle to make it harder work by turning the screw, which is why warders came to be called 'screws'.

Every aspect of life was severely ordered; the food followed a menu of tedious monotony. For example the standard diet ordered at the Somerset

Epiphany Sessions in January 1850 for those on hard labour for terms exceeding four months was as follows:

SUNDAY, TUESDAY, THURSDAY AND SATURDAY
Breakfast gruel 1 pint, bread 8 oz (M) 6 oz (F)
Dinner meat 4 oz (M) 3 oz (F), potatoes 1 lb (M) 8 oz (F), bread 6 oz

MONDAY, WEDNESDAY AND FRIDAY
Breakfast cocoa 1 pint, bread 8 oz (M) 6 oz (F)
Dinner soup 1 pint, bread 8 oz (M) 6 oz (F)
Supper gruel 1 pint, bread 8 oz (M) 6 oz (F)

The gruel was to contain 2 oz of oatmeal per pint, and on alternate days was to be sweetened with molasses or sugar and seasoned with salt. The meat was to be cooked and without any bone. The soup was to contain per pint 3 oz cooked meat without bone, 3 oz potatoes, 1 oz barley, rice or oatmeal, 1 oz of onion or leeks, and pepper and salt. The cocoa was to be made of 1 oz of flaked cocoa or cocoa nibs sweetened with 1 oz of molasses or sugar. Boys under fourteen were to have the female diet. Not exactly *haute cuisine*, but the soup sounds quite tasty.

The crank, for servitude. The prisoner had to turn the crank twenty times a minute for eight hours.

Looking back from today's perspective, life inside a Victorian prison sounds almost barbaric, but life outside could be even worse. There's a story of a flower girl who took off her shoe and deliberately smashed the lights outside the Mansion House, hoping to be arrested and thrown in gaol, because at least inside she would find shelter and food. In spite of the severe prison regime, during the 1840s about a quarter of inmates were re-offenders.

Gradually the authorities realised that solitude and servitude weren't really doing anyone any good, and that when convicts were released with no new skills they went straight back to their lives of crime. In the 1860s prison reformers won the case for supervised association between inmates, and a move towards 'useful' tasks. Some prisons started farms, others allowed inmates to learn the skills to sew uniforms and later mailbags; these were the first steps towards rehabilitation.

PLACES OF INTEREST

Armley Mills
Canal Road, Armley,
Leeds LS12 2QS
Tel: 01132 637861
www.leeds.gov.uk/torinfo
Victorian textile mills.

Barometer World
Quicksilver Barn
Merton, Okehampton,
Devon EX20 3DS
Tel: 01805 603443
www.barometerworld.com
Home of the 'tempest prognosticator'.

Beamish, The North of England
Open Air Museum
Beamish, Co. Durham DH9 0RG
Tel: 0191 370 4000
www.beamish.org.uk

Blackpool Central and North Piers
The Promenade, Blackpool
Tel: 01253 292029
www.blackpoollive.com

Blists Hill Victorian Museum
Blists Hill Victorian Town, Legges
Way, Madeley, Telford, TF7 5DU
Tel: 01952 433522
www.ironbridge.org.uk
Complete Victorian village to explore.

British Lawnmower Museum
106–114 Shakespeare Street,
Southport, Lancashire PR8 5AJ
Tel: 01704 501336
www.lawnmowerworld.co.uk

Brookwood Cemetery
Glade's House, Cemetery Pales,
Brookwood, Woking,
Surrey GU24 0BL
Tel: 01483 472 222
www.brookwoodcemetery.com/

Chard & District Museum
Godworthy House, High Street,
Chard, Somerset TA20 1QL
Tel: 01460 65091
(telephone for opening hours)
*John Stringfellow made the first powered
flight in a lace mill in Chard,
and the town museum has an exhibition
looking at his work.*

Cragside House, Garden & Estate
Rothbury
Morpeth

Northumberland NE65 7PX
Tel: 01669 620 150
www.nationaltrust.org

Down House
Luxted Road
Downe
Kent BR6 7JT
www.english-heritage.org.uk
Home of Charles Darwin.
Florence Nightingale Museum
2 Lambeth Palace Road,
London SE1 7EW
Tel: 020 7620 0374
www.florence-nightingale.co.uk

Fox Talbot Museum
Lacock, Nr Chippenham,
Wiltshire SN15 2LG
Tel: 01249 730227
www.fox-talbot.org.uk/fox-talbot
*The museum is in the grounds
of Lacock Abbey, home of pioneer
photographer Henry Talbot.*

Galleries of Justice
Shire Hall, High Pavement,
Lace Market,
Nottingham NG1 1HN
Tel: 0115 952 0555
www.galleriesofjustice.org.uk
*Exhibition of crime, punishment
and prisons through the ages.*

Gladstone Pottery Museum
Uttoxeter Road, Longton,
Stoke-on-Trent, ST3 1PQ
Tel: 01782 39232/311378
www.netcentral.co.uk/steveb/
museum/glad/index.htm
*Fine collection of Victorian plumbing
and artefacts.*

Great Western Railway Museum
Kemble Drive, Swindon SN2 2TA
Tel: 01793 466646
www.steam-museum.org.uk/
*Good collection of railway memorabilia,
especially Brunel.*

Great Western Society
Railway Centre, Didcot, OX11 7NJ
Tel: 01235 817200
Fax: 01235 510621
Email: didrlyc@globalnet.co.uk
www.didcotrailwaycentre.org.uk/
*Information on Brunel and the Great
Western Railway.*

Helmshore Textile Museum
Holcombe Road, Helmshore,
Rossendale, Lancs BB4 4NP
Tel: 01706 226459
Email: helmshoremuseum@
museumoflancs.org.uk
*This is the sister museum to
Queen Street Mill and deals with
other aspects of the cotton industry.*

HM Prison Service Museum
HM Prison Service College,
Newbold Revel, Nr Rugby,
Warwickshire CV23 0TH
Tel: 01788 834168/7
Email: museum@breathemail
www.hmprisonservice.gov.uk/
life/dynpage.asp?Page=144

Hollycombe Steam Collection
Iron Hill, Liphook, Hampshire,
GU30 7LP
Tel: 01428 724900
Email: hollycombe@talk21.com
www.hollycombe.co.uk
*Steam fair, steam trains and lots
of traction engines.*

Jack the Ripper casebook website
www.casebook.org/

Kew Bridge Steam Museum
Green Dragon Lane, Brentford,
Middlesex, TW8 0EN
Tel: 020 8568 4757
www.kbsm.org.uk

Kingston Museum
Wheatfield Way, Kingston upon
Thames, Surrey KT1 2PS
Tel: 0208 546 5386
Email: king.mus@rbk.kingston.gov.uk
www.kingston.gov.uk/museum/
Default.htm
*Muybridge bequeathed his collection of
plates, images, etc. to the Kingston Museum.*

Lanhydrock House
Lanhydrock, Bodmin,
Cornwall PL30 5AD
Tel: 01208 73320
www.nationaltrust.org.uk
Fine Victorian interiors.

Lawn Tennis Association Museum
The All England Lawn Tennis
and Croquet Club
Church Road, Wimbledon,
London SW19 5AE
Tel: 020 8946 6131
www.wimbledon.com/about/
museum.html

Manchester Museum of Science
and Industry
Liverpool Road, Castlefield,
Manchester, M3 4FP
Tel: 01618 322244
www.msim.org.uk
*Contains the original terminus of the
Liverpool & Manchester Railway.*

Museum of Iron
Darby Road, Coalbrookdale,
Ironbridge, Telford, TF8 7DX
Tel: 01952 433522
www.ironbridge.org.uk
*Includes special display on the Great
Exhibition of 1851.*

National Museum of Film,
Television and Photography
Pictureville, Bradford,
West Yorkshire, BD1 1NQ
Tel: 01274 202030
www.nmpft.org.uk

National Railway Museum
Leeman Road, York, Y026 4XJ
Tel: 01904 621261
www.nrm.org.uk

Natural History Museum
Cromwell Road, London, SW7 5BD
Tel: 020 7942 5000
www.nhm.ac.uk

Old Operating Theatre,
Museum & Herb Garret
9a St Thomas Street, Southwark,
London SE1 9RY
Tel: 020 7955 4791
www.thegarret.org.uk

Orient Express
Tel: 020 7805 5100
www.orient-expresstrains.com

Philpott Museum
Bridge Street, Lyme Regis, DT7 3QA
Tel: 01297 443370
www.lymeregismuseum.co.uk
Information on Mary Anning and fossils.

Porthcurno Museum
of Submarine Telegraphy
Eastern House, Porthcurno,
Cornwall, TR19 6JX
Tel: 01736 810 966
www.porthcurno.org.uk

Projection Box
easyweb.easynet.co.uk/
~s-herbert/ProjectionBox.htm
*Website dealing with the history
of moving pictures.*

Royal Geographical Society
1 Kensington Gore,
London, SW7 2AR
Tel: 020 7591 3000
www.rgs.org
Open to the public by appointment only.

Royal Institution
21 Albemarle Street,
London, W1S 4BS
Tel: 020 7409 2992
www.ri.ac.uk
Includes Michael Faraday's Laboratory.

Queen Street Mill
Textile Heritage Centre,
Queen Street, Harle Syke,
Burnley, BB10 2HX
Tel: 01282 412555
*The mill does not run every day,
so it is advisable to check opening times
before visiting.*

Royal Botanical Gardens, Kew
Richmond, Surrey TW9 3AB
Tel: 020 8332 5000
www.rbgkew.org.uk

Science Museum
South Kensington, Exhibition Road,
London SW7 2DD
Tel: 020 7942 4000
www.sciencemuseum.org.uk/

Sherlock Holmes Museum
221b Baker Street,
London NW1 6XE
Tel: 020 7935 8866
www.sherlock-
holmes.co.uk/home.htm

Sherlock links
www.sherlock-holmes.org/english.htm

Shuttleworth Collection
Old Warden Park
Near Biggleswade SG18 9EP
Tel: 01767 626 228
www.shuttleworth.org

Somerset Wildlife Trust
Fyne Court, Broomfield, Bridgwater,
Somerset TA5 2EQ
Tel: 01823 451 587
www.wildlifetrust.org.uk/
*Andrew Crosse lived here and it is possible
to see the room in which he conducted his
controversial experiments.*

SS *Great Britain*
Great Western Dock, Gas Ferry
Road, Bristol BS1 6TY
Tel: 0117 926 0680
Email: enquiries@ss-great-britain.com
www.ss-great-britain.com
*The ship is undergoing restoration
in the dock where she was built.*

Stringfellow website
www.john-stringfellow.com/

Swing Bridge
Newcastle-upon-Tyne
http://www.tyne-online.com/
history/history.html

Victoria and Albert Museum
Cromwell Road, South Kensington
London SW7 2RL
Tel: 020 7942 2000
www.vam.ac.uk

West Midlands Police Museum
Sparkhill Police Station
639 Stratford Road
Birmingham B11 4EA
Tel: 0121 626 7181
www.stvincent.ac.uk/Resources/
WMidPol/main.html

Willenhall Lock Museum
54/56 New Road, Willenhall,
West Midlands WV13 2DA
Tel: 01902 634 542

1837 Restaurant in Browns Hotel
Albemarle St, Mayfair,
London W1S 4BP
Tel: 020 7493 6020
www.brownshotel.com

Information on workhouses came
principally from the website of Peter
Higginbotham of Oxford University:
www.workhouses.org.uk

FURTHER READING

Bessemer, Henry, *Sir Henry Bessemer F.R.S.: An Autobiography*, Institute of Metals 1989

Brown, G.I., *The Guinness History of Inventions*, Guinness 1996

Corlett, Ewan, *The Iron Ship*, Conway Maritime Press 1990

Darwin, Charles, *(On) The Origin of Species by Means of Natural Selection*, John Murray 1859, Penguin 1968

Darwin, Charles, *The Voyage of the Beagle*, Wordsworth 1997

Davis, John R., *The Great Exhibition*, Sutton 1999

Derry, T.K and Trevor I. Williams, *A Short History of Technology*, Oxford U.P. 1960

Desmond, Adrian and James Moore, *Darwin*, Michael Joseph 1991, Penguin 1992

De Vries, Leonard, *Victorian Inventions*, John Murray 1971

Dougan, David, *The Great Gun-Maker: The Life of Lord Armstrong*, Frank Graham 1970

Fido, Martin and Keith Skinner, *The Official Encyclopedia of Scotland Yard*, Virgin 1999

Fort, Tom, *The Grass is Greener: Our Love Affair with the Lawn*, HarperCollins 2000

Grattan-Guinness, Ivor, *Psychical Research*, Aquarian Press 1982

Halliday, Stephen, *The Great Stink of London*, Sutton 1999

Inwood, Stephen, *A History of London*, Macmillan 1998

James, Frank A.J.L. (ed.), *Semaphores to Short Waves*, RSA 1998

Leapman, Michael, *The World for a Shilling: How the Great Exhibition of 1851 Shaped a Nation*, Headline 2001

Lyell, Charles, *Principles of Geology*, Penguin 1997

MacKenzie, John M. (ed.), *The Victorian Vision*, V&A Publications 2001

Petroski, Henry, *The Evolution of Useful Things*, Knopf 1992, Vintage Books 1994

Porter, Dale H., *The Life and Times of Goldsworthy Gurney*, Associated University Presses 1998

Priestley, Philip, *Victorian Prison Lives*, Pimlico 1999

Robertson, Patrick, *The Shell Book of Firsts*, Ebury Press & Michael Joseph 1975

Rolt, L.T.C., *Isambard Kingdom Brunel*, Longman 1957

Rolt, L.T.C., *Victorian Engineering*, Penguin 1970

Ronan, Colin A., *The Cambridge Illustrated History of the World's Science*, Cambridge University Press, 1983

Singer, Charles, *A History of Scientific Ideas*, Oxford University Press 1959

Thomas, Donald, *The Victorian Underworld*, John Murray 1998

Thomson, Keith S., *HMS Beagle*, Norton 1995

Vaughan, Adrian, *Isambard Kingdom Brunel*, Murray 1991

Weir, Robin, *et al.*, *Mrs Marshal: The Greatest Victorian Ice Cream Maker*, Smith Settle 1998

Index

27–41; brass powder 183; elevators 189; funfairs and rides 110, 114, 115; railways 10, 12, 23; steam engines 7, 22–3; *see also* mills; ploughs

steam turbines 39–41, 49

steamships 33–41, 187–8

steel 7, 183–5, 188, 189, 190

Stephenson, George 13, 40

Stephenson, Robert 10, 13, 81, 97

Stevens, John Cox 28

Stevenson, R.L. 52

Stoker, Abraham 52–3

Stone, Edward 155

Stoner, Capt. John Benjamin 93

storm prediction 93–5

Stringfellow, John 18–22, *20–1*

Stum, Charles 168

Sturgeon, William 49

surgery 8, 62–5

Swan, Joseph Wilson 192–4

swimming umbrellas and devices 32–3, *32*

table napkins 174

table tipping 69

Talbot, William Henry Fox 128, 129, *129*

Tavell, John 98

tea 154–5

telegrams 98, 103

telegraph 9, 96–7; electric 9, 49, 95–6, 97–103

telephone 98, 193

'tempest prognosticator' 93–4, *94*

theatres 115–21

Thomson, Robert 122

Thomson, William *see* Kelvin, Lord

tide tables 102

time ('railway time') 16

toys, with movement 130–1

traction engines 27

Trevithick, Richard 23

Tupper, Martin 79

Turbinia 40, 41

Tyndall, John 72

typhoid 8, 59, 61, 132, 144

tyres 122, 124

Ussher, Archbishop James 55

vélo-douche bicycle shower *133*, 135

Victoria, Queen *6*, 7–9, 155; birth of children 8, 63, 98; Buckingham Palace telegraph Station 9, 102; and Buffalo Bill 118; diamond jubilee 41; fired rifle 166, *167*; at the Great Exhibition 74–5, *76–7*, 84, 198; in a lift 190; photographs of 129; in Scotland 104, 106; train travel 8

Volta, Alessandro 48–9

Vulcan 29

vulcanite 157

Wallace, Alfred Russel 58, 84

wars 103

water-closets 8, 135, 141, 145, 147, 148, 149, 150

'water-frame' 23

Waterloo Station 66

'Waterloo teeth' 157, *157*

water supplies 8, 60–2, 132

Watson, Thomas 178

Watt, James 22, 39

weather maps and forecasts 94–5

Wedgwood, Tom 128

West Midlands Police Museum 208, *209*

Wheatstone, Charles 97, 99

Whewell, William 8

Whitney, Eli 165

Whitworth, Joseph 164–5; rifle 165–7, *166*, *167*

Whymper, Edward 72, *73*

Wick Lane sewer 142, *143*

Wilberforce, Samuel 59

Willenhall 196, 198, 202

Wimbledon 149; tennis 163

Wimshurst, James 49, 51, *51*

Wingfield, Walter Clopton 161–3

withdrawing rooms 126–7

workhouses 151–3

Wright brothers 18

Yale lock (Linus Yale Jr) 199, 202, *202*

'zoopraxiscope' 43
